The
OPAL
and the
PEARL

First published in 2017
by Columba Press
23 Merrion Square North,
Dublin 2, Co. Dublin
www.columba.ie

Copyright © 2016 Mark Patrick Hederman

ISBN: 978-1-78218-306-8

Set in Freight Text Pro 11/15
Cover and book design by Alba Esteban | Columba Press
Printed by ScandBook AB, Sweden

The
OPAL
and the
PEARL

MARK PATRICK
HEDERMAN

the columba press

Dedication:
To the ever-changing eleven
Who form a living
'S'
In the upper or lower room.

Let's get on with it

CONTENTS

Introduction

I am a monk. I have been sitting in a beautiful watch-tower for the last sixty years listening to whisperings of the world around me. Some of these promptings are contemporary; others come from the past. A monastery is a place where both can be gathered and connections can be made. Many people come to the monastery to tell their story, share their difficulties, offload their problems, and voice how the world wags for them. This gives insight into life as people live it. Every now and then the Holy Spirit points to an author or a work needing special attention. Such indication confers on that author or that work the significance of *Lectio Divina*, sacred reading which must be mulled over until it is understood. Here are four of the Irish authors assigned to me over the years; and here are the questions they pose to the architects of our living-space in the year 2017.

I find it a strange date. Almost like a brochure plucked out of science fiction, a stitch in time, since 'brochure' comes from the French word 'to stitch'. Here we are a hundred years on from the beginning of a dream; as if the future has caught up with us. We have no excuse for dawdling; the time is now. This is the beginning of the rest of our lives. Some are afraid of the future as a destructive hurricane off our coast. Others welcome it. Monks have a place in the fashioning of this future. They are guardians of air vents to an alternative world. There is always another possibility. Monks give breathing-space to a silent stuttering advisor trying to get a word in edgeways.

We need to harness a more comprehensive vision of the future, a more realistic awareness of our incapacity either to predict or make arrangements for what it will present. We are trying to prepare ourselves for a world we will never be able to forecast and never be required to inhabit. Every generation is a new continent never before explored. Only imagination can help us to prepare. Only imagination can sketch a possibility for seven billion people to live in harmony on this planet. How could any of us who grew up in the twentieth century have been prepared for the world of the twenty-first: a world of Text Twitter and Tweet?

Let us begin with a provocation: anyone who tells you what the future is going to be like is telling you a lie. There is no future laid out like a map. The future is what we make it. We can be told, and some are better than others at surmising, what is most likely to happen if we go on being the way we are, and others around us do likewise. Monks are there to keep open the road less travelled. Freewheeling down the auto route is too easy and too obvious; there may be a more wholesome way to negotiate the undergrowth, with more benefit to ourselves and less consequences for the paths we tread. Our country can continue to roll forward along the ebb and tide of randomness; or it can fuse with a larger and more comprehensive intentionality. Monks develop a capacity to understand in a certain way. Contemplation is the capacity to make connections where others may fail to see the point. Certain artists are also monks who have an added capacity to express what they perceive in a prophetic and irresistible rhythm, shape and form.

The future is not something out there which we step into as into an already designed space. The future is ourselves as we choose to become. Such a choice needs to meld with the world we inherit as we choose to arrange it. The future is alive with possibility to the extent that we are open to change. Change occurs most profitably in the wake of fundamental shifts in our way of being. These occur mostly because someone has imagined and described them.

How do we even begin to envisage such possibilities? Such vision of humanity and of the world it might inhabit is often the artist's task, sketching possible shapes for the future. There is no future as some kind of panorama laid out beforehand. The future does not exist until it happens. And we are the ones who make it happen. The future is neither a blank page nor is it an already designed house into which we are required to move. The future is what we build together, what we create together. Nor is it implemented in one deft and intelligent stroke. It occurs only at each moment, with the next move we make. And that can be original brainwave, or obdurate repetition of mistakes already made. We can become ugly, vulgar extensions of what we already are; or we can expand towards what we are being invited to become.

CHAPTER ONE

○

The Other Voice

The first half of the twentieth century was a battle for the 'soul' of Ireland. The Roman Catholic Church, as the century progressed, became the highest and the loudest bidder. This battle for the citadel became polarized into two camps: those defending Gaelic nationalism and those promoting cosmopolitan internationalism. Since most of the intelligentsia were protestant, it turned into a war between cultures. Spokespersons from each side, like AE and Shaw, on the one hand, and leading politicians, who publicly vaunted, in contrast, the fact that they were not intellectuals, on the other, presented almost contrary opposite views of the architecture of the new nation-state. Shaw called for the abandonment of nationalism saying that it must be added 'to the refuse pile of superstitions'. Anyone who wanted to divide the race into 'elect Irishmen' and 'reprobate foreign devils (especially Englishmen) had better go and live on the Blaskets where he can admire himself without much disturbance'. The Irish language was going to be a way of cutting off influence from outside, according to AE, who was afraid it was being used as 'a dyke behind which every kind of parochialism could shelter'. He wanted 'world culture, world ideas, world science; otherwise Ireland would not be a nation but a parish'. He used *The Irish Statesman*, founded in 1923, as a vehicle for his ideas. 'The cultural implications of the words *Sinn Féin* are evil', he wrote in 1925, 'We are not enough for ourselves. No race is. All learn from each other. All give to each other. We must not be afraid of world thought or world science. They will give vitality to our own nationality. If we shut the door against their entrance we shall perish intellectually, just as if we shut the door against the Gaelic we shall perish nationally'.

W.B. Yeats believed that the whole person, in the totality of every constituent part, was needed to discover and embody any worthwhile and reliable truth. He held that there is a religion which reneges on its responsibility to discover such truth and which becomes a search for immunity against the shocks of life. Such an impoverished religion was the one being proposed, in Yeats's view, for the New Ireland of the twentieth century. Such a fearful attempt to hide from the demands of human passion and human life was, for Yeats, a denial of the two essential mysteries of Christianity: Creation and Incarnation. One of the major differences between this earlier Christianity and the later manifestations of it, especially in the version being institutionalized in Ireland after independence, but also in various protestant variations, was its capacity to integrate the sexual as a sacred mystery central to all life of whatever kind. The character of Crazy Jane in Yeats's imagination represents the Old Testament of the Celtic race crying out against the bishop, representing institutionalized religion, especially its contemporary Irish Catholic variety. Sexual prudery and puritanism were major enemies in Yeats's crusade for a more integrated and wholesome Christianity.

The first ideology won a major victory in the Censorship of Publications Act of 1929, which also consolidated a connection between Church and State. Representatives of 'the other voice', such as W.B. Yeats and Bernard Shaw protested vehemently at the passing of this act. The new Republic was particularly single-minded in implementing its ideals. The Irish Free State in the twentieth century became an alignment of nationalist politics and the Roman Catholic Church. Two Eucharistic Congresses can act as bookends to the story being outlined: in 1932 the new aristocracy of Ireland were put on display as princes of the Church; the more recent Eucharistic Congress of 2012 as the second bookend could be said to close that chapter.

In 1937 the De Valera Constitution of our 'free' state, expressed this derivative philosophy. In a radio broadcast to the United States on 15 June that same year, De Valera called it 'the spiritual and cultural embodiment of the Irish people'. To mark its first anniversary in 1938, he reminded everybody, almost as in a sermon: 'as faith without good works is dead, so must we expect our Constitution to be if we are content to leave it merely as an idle statement of principles in which we profess belief but have not the will to put into practice'.

The message of artists to us, since the beginning of our new history, has been consistent and quite other. Their point of view has been repudiated or ignored by officialdom both in the church and in the state. The message might be summarized as follows: The picture of humanity that you are painting, whether in its ideal form, or in your perception of what it is actually like, is too narrow, too pessimistic, too 'other-worldly', too unsubtle. You refuse to accept the blood-and-guts reality of what we are, the bodily, sexual, earthy amalgam that makes us who we are. We want to be human, fully human. If God doesn't want our humanity the way it is, the way he made it, then he doesn't want us at all. He wants something else. The job of the artist is to describe, to express that reality as it actually is. Artists have been doing that from the beginning of our history as an independent state and because they have been doing that, they have been condemned, banned, excommunicated by the official organs of the Church and State.

'Somewhere in the nineteenth century' Patrick Kavanagh wrote in 1951, 'an anti-life heresy entered religion'.[1] Some of Kavanagh's poetry is an attack on the deeply pessimistic view of human nature perpetrated by the Catholic Church in Ireland, which he saw as 'anti-life' and which demanded that all his sexual energy 'be eliminated until expressed within the bonds of marriage'. Catholicism in Ireland was

1   *Kavanagh's Weekly*, 24 May, 1951.

a negation of incarnation and a blasphemy against creation. Church
and State were colluding in this necrophiliac distortion of Christianity. 'A wake is what is in progress in this country' and De Valera is the
undertaker 'in his long black cloak'.[2] His poem on Lough Derg is also
exploring 'the unresolved tension between flesh and spirit, between
life and anti-life, between joyous and sorrowful religion'.[3] John Jordan sees Kavanagh as one of the few Catholic writers who tries 'to
understand ... and treat with compassion' the prevailing 'perversion
of the Catholic teaching on sex and marriage'.[4]

If the Church can be seen as a defender of religious orthodoxy, art can become a champion of the orthodoxy of humanity. As
such it can take on either an individual or a collective voice. It can be
a protest against the way in which a whole group, a whole country,
a whole culture is leading its people. It can try to show us that as a
Western European Culture, as an Irish nation, or even as a particular community, we have been journeying on the Titanic for a whole
century, overconfident in the world-view, the infrastructure, the detailed management of daily life, that kept us afloat, and perilously
neglectful of all that was going on outside or below an apparently
subdued and tranquil surface. We could be heading for collision with
a perfectly natural ice-berg which we should have detected, assessed,
situated and negotiated, if we had been living in the real world which
not only surrounds us but actually is us.

Poetry as a personal and private language can be particularly
pioneering and exploratory in this regard. Ottavio Paz, the Mexican
writer, who won the Nobel Prize for literature in 1990, wrote a series
of 'Essays on Modern Poetry' called *The Other Voice*:

2   Ibid 10 May, 1952,
3   Una Agnew, *The Mystical Imagination of Patrick Kavanagh, A Buttonhole in Heaven*,
     Columba Press, Dublin, 1998, Pp 114-118.
4   John Jordan, 'Mr Kavanagh's Progress', *Studies*, Autumn, 1960.

That voice was not heeded by the revolutionary ideologues of our century, and this explains, in part at least, the cataclysmic failure of their plans. It would be disastrous if the new political philosophy were to ignore those realities that have been hidden and buried by the men and women of the Modern Age. The function of poetry for the last two hundred years has been to remind us of their existence; the poetry of tomorrow cannot do otherwise. Its mission will not be to provide new ideas but to announce what has been obstinately forgotten for centuries. Poetry is memory become image, and image become voice.[5]

Many have taken upon themselves the task of explaining and regulating the mystery of human life, few have had the opportunity of putting their ideas into practice. Situations such as The French Revolution, The American Declaration of Independence and the history of Russia since 1917, have provided scope and opportunity for the implementation of such ideologies. Our own situation in the Irish Republic, whatever one might feel or believe about its justification, its credibility or its ultimate viability, did provide for those responsible for constituting it, a unique and enviable opportunity to establish a cherishing and vitalizing environment for a manageable population on a relatively small-scale model. The question is: to what extent did they allow what we are here referring to as 'the other voice' to influence their architecture? And the answer to that question must be: not enough. In Ireland, art as the 'other voice', has been constant and assiduous in formulating a different, wider, less banal, and more variegated, identity than the one being prescribed for us by either Church or State. Far from the kind of dialogue between society and the arts, which would have been salutary and invigorating, an atmosphere of fear and suspicion developed. Creative interrogation and

5   Ottavio Paz, *The Other Voice, Essays on Modern Poetry,* Translated by Helen Lane, Harcourt, Brace, Jovanovich, 1991, Pp. 150-155.

criticism was silenced or ignored. Many artists protested vigorously, none more eloquently than George Bernard Shaw:

> In the nineteenth century all the world was concerned about Ireland. In the twentieth, nobody outside Ireland cares twopence what happens to her ... If, having broken England's grip of her, she slops back into the Atlantic as a little grass patch in which a few million moral cowards are not allowed to call their souls their own by a handful of morbid Catholics, mad with heresyphobia, unnaturally combining with a handful of Calvanists mad with sexphobia ... then the world will let 'these Irish' go their way into insignificance without the smallest concern.

Throughout our hundred year history we have been told the same thing in different ways by Edna O'Brien, John McGahern, for instance. Neither is saying there is no God, there is no Church, there is no Christianity. On the contrary, they are suggesting that if any of these realities want to have some effective contact with us and operate any kind of comprehensive salvation, they must begin taking seriously the partner with whom they are trying to have such a relationship. If we are to move forward towards a development which respects all the elements in the amalgam which we are, which we have become, which we hope to direct ourselves towards as an optimistic future, we must collaborate. Artists and scientists act as our antennae. They are diviners and creators of our future. They are our eyes, our ears, our imaginations. In the first part of this book I try to elaborate as clearly as I can what I have been hearing from four of our artists, two poets and two novelists.

CHAPTER TWO

◯

Joyce as Jesuit

There is a popular view that Joyce hated the Jesuits and had a particularly rough time at their hands. In fact, both he and his father had the highest opinion of the Jesuits. They were both snobs and they thought of the Jesuits as 'the Gentlemen of Catholic Education'. To quote James directly: 'I don't think you will easily find anyone to equal them'.[1] When in June 1891 John Joyce was forced, by straitened circumstances, to withdraw his son from Clongowes, he sent him to the Christian Brothers School in North Richmond Street. Not only is this fact not mentioned in *A Portrait of the Artist as a Young Man* but it was a source of shame to that artist and one which he took certain pains to obliterate from his biography.

The Christian Brothers were, in his father's phrase, 'Paddy Stink and Mickey Mud' and however unflattering a picture emerges from Joyce's description of his sojourn in Clongowes, it is at least regarded as worthy of mention. In 1895, after James had won two exhibitions in the Intermediate examination, the Joyces were approached by the Dominicans who offered James free board and tuition at their school. By this time James had been reassigned to the Jesuits in Belvedere College, thanks to a happy meeting between John Joyce and the former rector of Clongowes, Fr Conmee, who had been appointed rector of Belvedere and who was anxious to help out his former student, fallen on hard times. When the offer came from the Dominicans, John Joyce left the decision to his son. James declared without hesitation, 'I began with the Jesuits and I want to end with them'.[2]

....
1   Richard Ellmann, *James Joyce*, The First Revision of the 1959 Classic, OUP 1983, p. 27.
2   Ibid, p. 475.

Harriet Shaw Weaver wrote to Joyce about the Nausicaa episode of *Ulysses* saying: 'You are very good for the soul, I think, medicinal, you are so unflattering to our human nature: So, though you are neither priest nor doctor of medicine, I think you have something of both – the Reverend James Joyce, S.J., M.D'.[3] And Joyce himself once corrected Frank Budgen by remarking: 'You allude to me as a Catholic. Now for the sake of precision and to get the correct contour on me, you ought to allude to me as a Jesuit'.[4]

The Jesuits had an influence on Joyce, not just as educators but as archetypes. As educators they taught him, again in his own words, 'to arrange things in such a way that they become easy to survey and to judge';[5] as archetypes they provided the framework within which the portrait of the artist was eventually to emerge. In a moving letter to Lady Gregory in November 1902, asking her for money as was his wont, Joyce at the age of twenty, describes himself as a 'misbeliever' but one of great faith: 'All things are inconstant except the faith in the soul, which changes all things and fills their inconstancy with light. And though I seem to have been driven out of my country here as a misbeliever I have found no man yet with a faith like mine'.[6] A misbeliever is somewhere between a believer and an unbeliever. Writing to Nora on the 29 August 1904, he says: 'Six years ago I left the Catholic Church, hating it most fervently. I found it impossible for me to remain in it on account of the impulses of my nature. I made secret war upon it when I was a student and declined to accept the positions it offered me. By doing this I made myself a beggar but I retained my pride. Now I make open war upon it by what I write and say and do'.[7] His brother Stanislaus gives the following analysis:

---

3   Ibid. p. 27.
4   Ibid.
5   Louis Golding, *James Joyce,* London, 1933, p. 55.
6   Richard Ellmann, ed., *Selected Letters,* The Viking Press, New York, 1975, p.8.
7   Ibid Pp. 25-26.

My brother's breakaway from Catholicism was due to other motives. He felt it was imperative that he should save his real spiritual life from being overlaid and crushed by a false one that he had outgrown. He believed that poets in the measure of their gifts and personality were the repositories of the genuine spiritual life of their race and the priests were usurpers. He detested falsity and believed in individual freedom more thoroughly than any man I have ever known. [...] The interest that my brother always retained in the philosophy of the Catholic Church sprang from the fact that he considered Catholic philosophy to be the most coherent attempt to establish such an intellectual and material stability.[8]

There are many arguments about whether Joyce was a 'Catholic' writer, whether he ever actually left the Catholic Church, whether he believed in God.[9] It seems to me that the only religion he took seriously was the Catholic faith which was forcefully presented to him during his childhood. He rejected this faith in the way it was presented, but this does not mean that he rejected the whole theological project of saving humanity and putting it in relationship with God, if all these terms were correctly understood. In Chapter Five of *A Portrait* Cranly asks Stephen if, having lost his faith in the Catholic Church, he might not consider becoming a Protestant. 'I said that I had lost the faith', Stephen answered, 'but not that I had lost self-respect. What kind of liberation would that be to forsake an absurdity which is logical and coherent and to embrace one which is illogical and incoherent?'

It seems quite likely that Joyce could have been persuaded to become a Jesuit but for one essential element in his make-up which pre-

8   Stanislaus Joyce, *My Brother's Keeper*, London: Faber and Faber, 1982, p 120.
9   Geert Lernout, *Help My Unbelief: James Joyce and Religion*, Continuum, London, 2010, gives an intelligent and readable summary of most of the arguments to date.

cluded this possibility. Quite early in the career of Stephen Dedalus, as this unfolds in *A Portrait*, we are given several indications about his sense of vocation. The director of Belvedere College questioned him very seriously on this score, and the whole movement of *A Portrait* carries the soul of Stephen Dedalus along two paths, 'the path of the priest he might have been and the path of the artist he is to become'.[10] Boys of his intelligence and sensitivity were often coaxed into the Order. One early commentator says 'it is in fact rather in the direction of intellectual curiosity than of single piety that he is different from other boys, but it is precisely out of such material that priests are made – and heretics'.[11]

The one element in his personality which prevented this possible outcome was his unusually precocious sexuality. For a boy of his age in a Dublin day-school he seems to have had considerable sexual experience. His sexuality formed the warring partner in the struggle towards his ultimate destiny. He realised that the call to the priesthood meant the eradication of this aspect of himself. He saw the Catholic Church as a call to a certain kind of perfection which demanded emasculation and evisceration.

A Portrait of the Artist as a Young Man describes the bitter and lonely struggle between these two warring elements in an almost unbearably sensitive youth. The famous sermon on hell was the final blow to his possible vocation to the priesthood. 'Before the rector had delivered himself of his last word, the developing priest was slain in Stephen Dedalus; the developing artist, like a waiting animal, stared watchfully and did not move'.[12]

Joyce decided to remain true to his own nature and to reject the way of life proposed to him, and endorsed by all who surrounded him. This involved the three famous rejections of family, faith and

10   Louis Golding, *James Joyce*, London, 1933, p. 55
11   Ibid.
12   Ibid. p. 56.

fatherland.[13] His mind began to 'feel its way towards some comprehension of the actual nature and dimensions of the work imposed upon him by his own nature and qualities'.[14]

From the beginning Joyce thought of himself as a poet. His first artistic attempts were poems which he later published in two volumes *Chamber Music* and *Pomes Penyeach*.[15] It is also clear from a reading of these works that he was a mediocre poet. Some of his poems are weak and syrupy, others no more than doggerel. However, as Louis Golding perceptively pointed out, as far back as 1933, these poems still hold the key to Joyce the artist. As his first attempts to undertake his work as an artist, they incarnate the purest and deepest of his longings in this regard. In his life as an artist Joyce tried every form of artistic literary expression and if he ended up having to invent his own, this was because he realised that he could never be an adequate poet and yet he could not renounce his aspirations towards a creativity which would incorporate his essentially lyrical impulse. It is Golding's contention that the intensely fearsome struggle which Joyce underwent as a boy in a Jesuit boarding school not only burnt out of him any aspiration towards a priestly vocation but also cauterized any possibility of becoming a poet. In this regard it is interesting to note how many of the poets of Ireland were educated and brought up in a Protestant atmosphere. The ethos of Catholicism in Ireland at this time was bullying and insensitive. It is the irrepressible Buck Mulligan who explains this secret to us in one of his more serious descriptions of Stephen in *Ulysses*:[16]

13   "When a man is born...there are nets flung at it to hold it back from flight. You talk to me of nationality, language, religion. I shall try to fly by those nets." "This race and this country and this life produced me, he said. I shall express myself as I am." [quotations from Chapter Five of *A portrait of the artist as a young man*.]

14   Louis Golding, op. cit. p 35.

15   *Chamber Music* first published in 1907; *Pomes Penyeach* first published in 1927. Both are contained in The Essential James Joyce, ed. Harry Levin, Triad/Panther Paperback, 1977.

16   *Ulysses*, 1958 edition, p. 236.

They drove his wits astray, he said, by visions of hell. He will never capture the Attic note. The note of Swinburne, of all poets, the white death and the ruddy birth. That is his tragedy. He can never be a poet. The joy of creation...

By the end of *A Portrait* it is clear that Stephen's education has made him a rebel.[17]

I will tell you what I will do and what I will not do. I will not serve that in which I no longer believe, whether it call itself my home, my fatherland or my church: and I will try to express myself in some mode of life or act as freely as I can and as wholly as I can, using for my defence the only arms I allow myself to use, silence, exile and cunning.

Lieutenant-Colonel P.R. Butler, an exact contemporary of Joyce in Clongowes, recalls that 'each pupil had to make a recitation chosen for its real or fancied appositeness to his own character. Butler's piece was "The Charge of the Light Brigade" while Joyce's was "Little Jim", which begins,

The cottage was a thatched one
its outside old and mean,
but everything within that cot
was wondrous neat and clean.

and ends with the prayer of the dying Jim's parents,

in heaven once more to meet
their own poor little Jim.

....
17   *A Portrait of the Artist as a Young Man*. Last paragraph.

The mawkishness was not lost upon either the scornful listeners or the embarrassed reciter'.[18]

This 'little Jim' who was shattered and paralysed by the grim world in which he found himself was the poet that Joyce could never become. Artistic life became the creative attempt to pick up these pieces and give expression to the survivor. His poetry contains the secret of his fundamental aspiration. But this secret never found adequate expression in the medium of poetry for reasons that are again sensitively analysed by Louis Golding:[19]

> I say of poetry that it is the exercise of the subconscious mind, because, whatever the source of it, the element of irresponsibility is stronger in poetry than in any other forms of aesthetic composition in words, even though the conscious mind may quite scientifically, throughout the whole process, organise the technique of its expression. That Stephen Dedalus did not give up all hope that he might some day exercise in poetry the subconscious mind is proved by the pathetic retention of the scraps of verse which constitute *Pomes Penyeach*. It is as if he hoped that by muttering them over to himself he might some day suddenly, in the fortunate coincidence of cabbalistic syllables, find that the iron doors opposed to him had drawn apart.

The loss of Joyce the poet gave birth to Joyce the artist. He had to consciously set about constructing a way of expressing himself and this detour forced him to become one of the most important artificers of all time. If he could not be a poet he could, at least, describe the contours of this paralysis and, in so doing, perhaps release himself from his own cocoon.

---

18   Richard Ellmann, *James Joyce*, 1983 op. cit., p. 31.
19   Louis Golding, op. cit., p. 20.

The three sources of paralysis from which Joyce sought to liberate us and himself were family, faith, and fatherland: three nets which ensnared the people of Ireland. He described such paralysis in its various forms in *Dubliners*. 'I am writing a series of *epicleti* – ten – for a paper. I have written one. I call the series *Dubliners* to betray the soul of that hemiplegia or paralysis which many consider a city'.[20] He wrote to his reluctant publisher, Grant Richards in 1906: 'My intention was to write a chapter in the moral history of my country and I chose Dublin for the scene because that city seemed to me the centre of paralysis'.[21] *Ulysses* began as one of those short stories. It was to consider a moment when he had been saved from a mugging by a kindly older man. The story was to be called 'Mr Hunter's Day', or 'Ulysses in Dublin', but as Joyce wrote in a letter to his brother Stanislaus (6 Feb. 1907): it 'never got forrader than the title'.[22] '[Ulysses] is the epic of two races (Israel – Ireland) and at the same time the cycle of the human body as well as a little story of a day (life). The character of Ulysses always fascinated me ever since boyhood. I started writing it as a short story for *Dubliners*, fifteen years ago but gave it up. For seven years I have been working at this book – blast it!'[23] 'It was the book of my youth [...] but *Ulysses* is the book of my maturity, and I prefer my maturity to my youth. *Ulysses* is more satisfying and better resolved; for youth is a time of torment in which you can see nothing clearly. But in *Ulysses* I have tried to see life clearly, I think, and as a whole; for *Ulysses* was always my hero. Yes, even in my tormented youth, but it has taken me half a lifetime to reach the necessary equilibrium to express it, for my youth was exceptionally violent; painful and violent'.[24]

20   Letter to Curran of early 1904, in *Letters*, I, p.55; *Selected Letters*, 1975, p.22..
21   Richard Ellmann, ed., *Selected Letters*, 1975, p.83.
22   *Selected Letters*, Faber 1975, p.145.
23   Letter to Carlo Linati, 21 Sept. 1920, in *Selected Letters*, 1975, p.270-71 [given in Italian with an unattributed translation in a footnote, being n.1, p.271]
24   Arthur Power, *Conversations with James Joyce*, London; Millington 1974, pp.36-37.

Clive Hart suggests that Joyce's works are all in the nature of self-purgation and that each of his books are 'the expression of a sensibility haunted by emotional conflicts requiring the most powerful symbolic exorcism. This personal – often uncomfortably personal – art was the only kind Joyce could create or understand ... As soon as the personal experience had been externalized ... the drives and conflicts temporarily evaporated and interest dissolved ... Whenever the need for artistic purgation arose again, fresh techniques were necessary; the same magic could not be made to work twice. On each occasion a more potent exorcism was called for, involving greater complexity, more difficult labyrinths from which to escape, and, above all, the objectification and rationalisation of more and more personal involvement'.[25]

Whatever about Joyce's poetry, his novels are hailed as masterpieces of that art form. Some would claim that Joyce is the greatest novelist of the twentieth century and that *Ulysses* is one of the outstanding novels of all time. Be that as it may, it was not really what interested Joyce. He was a novelist by default and some would say that this period of his artistic career was no more than the necessary therapeutic interval which allowed him to resume his original poetic impulse in his final work *Finnegans Wake*.

To the connoisseurs of the aesthetic form of the novel his last work is an aberration. It marks eighteen years of senile decay during which the novelist of our time wasted his talent and his time concocting a huge labyrinthine joke in bad taste.[26] To take such a point of view is to misunderstand this particular artistic project. Joyce was not interested in art for art's sake. Art, for him, was the indispensable medium through which he could give expression to himself. The fact that he was an incomparable master of the technique of the novelist did not allow him to bask in the glory of such virtuosity.

25   Clive Hart, *Structure and Motif in Finnegans Wake*, Faber, London, 1962, p 25-26.
26   cf for example Stan Gebler Davies who takes this point of view.

Joyce's work must be seen as a whole. His was a life in search of 'the word': not the word of incarnation which would allow his word to be made flesh in the most satisfying and aesthetically pleasing form, but the word of resurrection – his flesh made word and restored to life. For Joyce the word was life and the problem which haunted him and which made him change so often his literary forms was how best to become consubstantial with that word. This is the theme of the famous Hamlet discussion in *Ulysses*. It is the theme of creativity, not as causality but as paternity. Joyce's aesthetic was far nearer to that of Thomas Aquinas than is generally allowed by most commentators. This is not because the words he uses are borrowed from 'the bulldog of Aquin' but because the context in which he uses them implies a similar preoccupation. The famous definition of beauty in terms of *integritas, claritas* and *consonantia*, which have been removed from their original context and developed into a supposedly Thomistic aesthetic were never originally intended as such. St Thomas would have been amazed to find this particular aspect of his reflection transformed into the cornerstone for a philosophy which hardly concerned him. The point which Aquinas seeks to establish is a theological one: an image or *similitudo* is beautiful if it perfectly represents another being, especially if that being is the sum total of all perfection. It is in this sense that the Son, as the second person of the Trinity must be conceived [in every sense of the word]. He thereby has a special, if not exclusive, title to the divine name: beauty.[27]

These remarks of Aquinas on beauty occur in an argument for the suitability of applying to the person of the Son in the uncreated Trinity a particular attribute or name.[28] The beauty of the Son as the Word of God is his capacity to embody, to represent, to incarnate his originating principle. The beauty of Joyce's work would be its capac-

---

27   William T. Noon, S.J., *Joyce and Aquinas*, YUP, 1957, p. 105f.
28   Thomas Aquinas, *Summa Theologiae*, I, q.39.a.8.

ity to realise the perfection of itself as work of art, and of its author as the one seeking such perfect self-expression.

In 1949 Louis Gillet, a friend and contemporary of Joyce, suggested that 'the problem of paternity ... is the essential basis of the Joyce problem, the one that explains in *Ulysses* ... the long meditation of Stephen and Mulligan on the subject of Hamlet. In fact this fragment is the key to the book ... (It can never be sufficiently emphasised to what extent this astonishing play constitutes the real source of Joyce's work ... even, prefigured by the scenes of humour and lunacy, the monumental madness of *Finnegans Wake*)'.[29] Paternity, for Joyce, means not only the relationship between father and son but also the relationship between the artist and his work. Such a relationship finds its aesthetic paradigm in Shakespeare's Hamlet and its supreme analogy in the word of an all-powerful creator. Joyce's own creativity had no less an analogy in view. His only rival in the field was Shakespeare, his only possible superior, if he existed at all, was the God of creation. These were the lions he was proud to hunt.

Thomas Aquinas combines the two strands of art and fatherhood in his presentation of the mysterious relationship which exists between the Father and the Son (the uncreated principle and the consubstantial word). Thomas was aware of all the heresies which threatened the fullness and the subtlety of so delicately balanced a mystery. Of these the two most representative would be Arianism and Sabellianism, both of which feature constantly in Stephen's thought in *Ulysses* and *A Portrait*. The first denies the possibility of fatherhood in God. The son was very similar and 'of like substance' (*homoiousios*) but could never be 'consubstantial' (*homoousios*) with God. This implied, from Joyce's point of view, that any word or creation of his own could never be the perfect form of himself. He was more attracted to 'the subtle African heresiarch Sabellius who held

29 Louis Gillet, 'Stele for James Joyce', *James Joyce Yearbook*, Paris, 1949, pp.42-43.

that the Father was Himself His own Son'.[30] This heresy, sometimes called Modalism or Monarchianism (that to preserve the prerogatives of Divine Monarch it is necessary to present the son as no more than a ghost, or a modality, of the Father) is dramatised in Shakespeare's *Hamlet*. It is this Sabellian notion of creativity which is represented by Stephen in *Ulysses* and it is only after the odyssey of this work of art that a new definition of fatherhood is achieved in the person of Leopold Bloom.

This apparently abstruse theological argument is important in that it situates the source and the goal of Joyce's art outside the realisation and perfection of that art in and for itself. Joyce's life and work were a dedicated search and struggle in another order. His goal was a kind of self-expression which would exorcise, by complete and satisfactory embodiment, the demons haunting his own life. It also shows that no work of Joyce can be understood as an isolated entity. To say that *Ulysses* was the best and only really great work that Joyce ever produced, and to discard the rest on this account, may be permissible in the domain of aesthetic criticism but it is impossible in the context of Joyce's overall project.

Of course it is important to appraise the role of Joyce the novelist, but not before situating this novelist within the wider context of an artistic odyssey which begins with *Chamber Music* and culminates and finds its fulfilment in *Finnegans Wake*. However 'good' the other works may or may not be, they are episodes on the way towards the only really important thing. This important thing is *Finnegans Wake* which is the same thing as *Chamber Music* except that here that original urge has become word made flesh. As Samuel Beckett in his famous essay on *Finnegans Wake* tells us: 'Here form is content, content is form. You complain that this stuff is not written in English. It is not written at all. It is not to be read – or rather it is (not) only to

30 *Ulysses*, p 18.

be read. It is to be looked at and listened to. His writing is not about something; it is that something itself'.[31]

Nobody, at the time, of his friends, his family, his critics, his admirers, approved of, or understood, what he was doing in *Finnegans Wake*, this 'work in progress' as he called it, until the day when its secret title was revealed. All of Joyce's life was a 'work in progress'. This last was the culmination of that lifetime's odyssey and holds the key to any understanding of Joyce himself.

Harriet Shaw Weaver, on whom Joyce depended so ignominiously and ruthlessly, was completely disenchanted by this work. Joyce took great pains to explain to her the importance of it and in the end succeeded in bludgeoning her into submission. His brother Stanislaus was quite clear that 'I for one would not read more than a paragraph of it, if I did not know you'. He suspects that 'the drivelling rigmarole' in the 'nightmare production' is written 'with the deliberate intention of pulling the reader's leg'.[32] H.G. Wells spoke for most as follows:[33]

> Now with regard to this literary experiment of yours. It's a considerable thing because you are a very considerable man and you have in your crowded composition a mighty genius for expression which has escaped discipline. But I don't think it gets anywhere. You have turned your back on common men, on their elementary needs and their restricted time and intelligence and you have elaborated. What is the result? Vast riddles ... So I ask: Who the hell is this Joyce who demands so many waking hours of the few thousands I have still to live for a proper appreciation of his quirks and fancies and flashes of rendering?

31   Samuel Beckett, 'Dante ... Bruno ... Vico ... Joyce' in *Our Examination Round His Factification for Incamination of Work in Progress*, Faber & Faber, 1929. This essay is reproduced in *A Bash in the Tunnel*, ed. John Ryan cf p. 28 for the above quotation.
32   Letter from Stanislaus dated August 7, 1924, reproduced in *Selected Joyce Letters* edited by Richard Ellmann, New York, 1975, p. 589.
33   Letter from H.G. Wells dated November 15, 1926, in Ellmann op. cit., p. 597.

Ezra Pound, who might have been the person most likely to understand Joyce's art, has this to say after reading a typescript of one chapter: 'Nothing would be worth plowing through this, except the Divine Vision – and I gather it's not that sort of thing'.[34] So, in fact, he was alone in his struggle during the eighteen years that it took him to compose his final work.

The questions of Pound and Wells: 'Who is this Joyce? What is this vision?' are still the important ones to answer before finding our way through the labyrinth. There must be many people who read James Joyce for pleasure and this is obviously one very good reason for doing so. I have never found him easy or pleasurable to read. I read him because I have to, because I believe that, as Richard Ellmann says in the opening line of his biography: 'We are still learning to be James Joyce's contemporaries'.

If the poet Milton felt called upon to explain the ways of God to humankind, Joyce felt obliged to explain the ways of humankind to God. Having rejected the orthodoxy of the Catholic Church he embraced with passion and rigour the orthodoxy of humanity. He realized that there was more to humanity than Jesuit philosophy had ever dreamed of, and was determined to explore that dream. The first essential step in that direction is contained in his novel *Ulysses*.

> On that occasion we gave a small dinner at our home in Paris.... The birthday cake was decorated with an ingenious candy replica of a copy of *Ulysses*, in its blue jacket. Called on to cut the cake, Joyce looked at it a moment and said: *Accipite et manducate ex hoc omnes: Hoc est enim corpus meum!*[35]

---

34 Letter from Ezra Pound dated November 15, 1926 in Ellmann op. cit., p. 597.
35 Eugene Jolas, in My Friend James Joyce: quoted in A. M. Klein, "The Black Panther," Accent, X (1950), p. 154.

Part of his overall project was his understanding of the real meaning of the Eucharist, as this had been instituted by Jesus Christ, the word made flesh and then once again become word. Joyce believed that the Catholic Church had reduced and deformed that magnificent reality and he set about restoring its comprehensive originality in his work.

To understand the true significance of Joyce's last work, *Finnegans Wake*, which was not a novel, it is important to understand the internal conflict which he used the novel form to exorcise in *Ulysses*. Joyce turned to the novel as a substitute for poetry, as the only other artistic medium available to him. Although he was exceptionally gifted in this art form he did not respectfully submit to the established canons of 'the Great Tradition' in novel writing. On the contrary, having abandoned religion and science as methods of self-expression he was hardly likely to find anything satisfactory readily available. The reason he turned to art was precisely because it afforded him the opportunity of recreating the forms necessary for expressing his originality. In the field of novel writing he found exactly the same weaknesses and prejudices he had found in the world around him. He not only revolutionised the form of the novel, but he exploited this medium for the purpose of displaying the paralysis which enveloped every aspect of life in Ireland, including art itself. His project was to exorcise himself from the impossibilities of becoming a poet by expressing in the most perfect form these very impossibilities.

The major weakness of the novel, from Joyce's point of view, was that it had turned itself into a kind of science. The text was a highly controlled story which both the reader and the writer were able to dominate. The form which imposes this pattern of meaning from beginning to end is the narrative. Here the reader is aware that the author is telling the story and forcing the reader to submit to this guiding hand. The text is the perfectly predictable third term between the reader and the writer and it is governed by a series of conventions which prevent any unnecessary straying on the part of the reader.

All the novelists of the Great Tradition leading to the twentieth century carefully tie the reader into a chair and imperiously force feed their story without any movement of, or participation from, their captive audience. Dictatorial monologue is the idiom of the novel and the successful novelist is the one who best knows how to hypnotise and anaesthetize the subservient reader. Obviously, the author introduces voices other than his or her own into the text. But these are carefully cordoned off between inverted commas, which Joyce regarded as 'perverted commas', and thus prevented from assuming any life of their own. The real language of the text is the narrative proper which is impregnated with the meta-language of a smug and all-pervading commentary by the author, who speaks directly to the reader and removes all the threat and the obscurity from the other discourses which are quoted as mere illustrations of his/her basic text. This domination of the author is the tyranny of the father-figure which precludes any active participation of the reader outside the carefully controlled manipulation of the narrative. It removes all responsibility, in the sense of creative and personal reaction. It reduces the reader to a dull passivity. It also deprives language of its own specific life. It forces it into a linear strait-jacket of predetermined meaning. It allows the author to use both language and the reader as lifeless robots.

The revolution of the word[36] which Joyce achieved was the liberation of both language and the reader by his renunciation of any dominating vantage-point as author of the text. When we read *Dubliners*, for instance, we are never able to establish the identity of the subject who is telling the story. 'It has been argued that the general strategy of *Dubliners* is the refusal of the production of a

------

36   Colin McCabe, *James Joyce & the Revolution of the Word*, London, MacMillan, 1978.

privileged discourse against which to read off the other languages of the text. This refusal forces the reader to experience the discourses of the characters as articulation rather than representation; in short to experience language'.[37]

'Both *Ulysses* and *Finnegans Wake* are concerned not with representing experience through language but with experiencing language through a destruction of representation ... Joyce's text disrupts the normal position assigned to a reader in a text and thus alters the reader's relation to his or her discourses'.[38] Joyce is trying to alter the established relationships between an author and a reader through the material vehicle of words. The confident 'I' of the author is silenced to allow something else to speak. This something else is the mystery of language itself. The word ceases to be a transparent nonentity through which the reader is made aware of another, exterior and 'real' world, and becomes a reality with a life of its own.

The revolution of the word was not just undertaken for its own sake. It was necessary for Joyce himself. As author he had no self-confident self which could act as privileged narrator of his text. Allowing language its freedom opened for him the possibility of finding his own voice rather than imposing it from the outset. In fact there were several voices in him, all of which achieve articulation in the deconstructed narrative which becomes a tapestry of interlocking discourse. More importantly, language could release Joyce himself from imprisonment within his own intestines.

Two aspects of Joyce's life are also present in his letters and they represent the two dimensions of puritanical religious upbringing and highly developed sexual instinct, which for many people create a particularly 'Catholic' temperament. These two 'types' are incarnated in Stephen and Bloom and the whole structure of the novel, especially the Scylla and Charybdis episode, is based upon the distinc-

37 Ibid p 54.
38 Ibid Pp 4-5

tion between body and soul, matter and spirit. For Joyce the sexual dimension is fundamental and defines the being of a character and, at this level, either excessive materialism or excessive spirituality is destructive. In this sense he was a contemporary in spirit of the Surrealists, of Proust, of Freud, of Jung, of Rilke and those who sensed the new dimensions which were opening up to humanity. Not that he was in anyway appreciative of his contemporaries. He despised Freud and Jung, for example, referring to them as 'Tweedledum and Tweedledee'. He felt that they were pillaging a reality which artists alone were capable of expressing, and exploiting it for their own particular practical needs. They were reducing it to the limited categories of their own minds and training, whereas he was opening himself and allowing this reality to spread through him so that every organ, channel, category, or compartment, was flooded. Invasion from the unconscious hardened and captured by words became the volcano which erupted in the being of the artist and displayed itself in the larva left behind after the explosion.

The reason why Joyce had to use the style he eventually forged for himself in *Finnegans Wake* is because 'one great part of every human existence is passed in a state which cannot be rendered sensible by the use of wideawake language, cut-and-dry grammar and go-ahead plot' as he wrote back to Ezra Pound.[39] Lionel Trilling held that 'James Joyce, with his interest in the numerous states of receding consciousness, with his use of words which point to more than one thing, with his pervading sense of the interrelation and interpenetration of all things, and, not least important, his treatment of familial themes, has perhaps most thoroughly and consciously exploited Freud's ideas'.[40] This is not to imply that he was directly influenced by Freud's writings. As Lionel Trilling again points out: 'We must see that particular influences cannot be in question here but that what

39   *Selected Joyce Letters* edited by Richard Ellmann, New York, 1975, p. 597.
40   Lionel Trilling, *The Liberal Imagination*, London, Secker & Warburg, 1951, p. 40.

we must deal with is nothing less than a whole *Zeitgeist*, a direction of thought'.[41] When Freud was hailed, on the occasion of his seventieth birthday, as 'the discoverer of the unconscious', he corrected the speaker and refused the title: 'The poets and philosophers before me discovered the unconscious. What I discovered was the scientific method by which the unconscious can be studied'.[42]

And it was precisely this scientific method which Joyce rejected when facing the unconscious. He dismissed psychoanalysis because its symbolism was mechanical,[43] but this was surely because, as Ellmann suggests, 'Joyce was close to the new psychoanalysis at so many points that he always disavowed any interest in it'.[44] He was in fact working along the same lines himself at an artistic level and was disdainful of the plodding scientists who were tapping the same sources in a much less direct and revealing way. Art was the only appropriate medium for Joyce. Medicine and science were half measures which were even less satisfactory than the religion which he had rejected. Talking about psychoanalysis he said to his friend Ettore Schmitz: 'Well, if we need it, let us keep to confession'.[45] But, at another level, the level of coincidence, corresponding to the suggestion of Trilling about the *Zeitgeist*, which influenced him to an extent which has not yet been fully appreciated, he realised that his work was very definitely connected to that of both Freud and Jung.

What is it that all these people were discovering? The answer is an inner continent, the discovery of which had greater significance and repercussion than the discovery of the 'New World' by Europeans in the fifteenth century. The difference between Joyce and the psychoanalysts, for instance, was that he was discovering as an artist and therefore sought to express this reality in all its originality,

41 Ibid. p 35.
42 Ibid p. 34.
43 Ellmann, *James Joyce* (1983) op. cit., p. 382.
44 Ibid. p 436.
45 Ibid. p 472.

subtlety and polyvalence, whereas they, as scientists sought to conquer it by reducing it to the machinery available to their limited fields of competence. 'In *Ulysses*, I have recorded, simultaneously, what a man says, sees, thinks, and what such saying, seeing and thinking does, to what you Freudians call the subconscious – but as for psychoanalysis, it's neither more nor less than blackmail'.[46] Joyce described *Finnegans Wake* as written 'to suit the esthetic of the dream, where the forms prolong and multiply themselves, where the visions pass from the trivial to the apocalyptic, where the brain uses the roots of vocables to make others from them which will be capable of naming its phantasms, its allergies, its illusions'.[47]

His search was in a similar direction and dimension to that of the doctors and scientists, investigating the inner world of dreams and of the unconscious. What he disliked was their methodology. When asked by the Danish writer Tom Kristensen to provide some help in the interpretation of his Work in Progress, Joyce referred him to Vico. Kristensen asked him if he believed in the Scienza Nuova. Joyce replied: 'I don't believe in any science, but my imagination grows when I read Vico as it doesn't when I read Freud and Jung'.[48]

Such remarks are important for an understanding of precisely how writers and thinkers influenced Joyce's work, stressing a difference between scientific and artistic discovery. The first has its identifiable and identifying equipment with which it can harness the new reality. This equipment is a fixed immovable third term between the scientist and the object of science. The precast forms into which the new reality is required to pour itself, have not only a sterilizing effect upon it but they also ensure that the scientists are never threatened, to the extent of total transformation of their own reality, by any newness which may confront them. Artists have no preconceived forms

....
46   Ibid. p 524.
47   Ibid. p 546.
48   Ibid. p 693

or approaches. They have to give themselves totally to the newness which they sense, and then invent the forms which alone can give that reality concrete expression.

Joyce rejected both religious and scientific pretensions to monopoly in the area of human understanding. The new world which had been discovered required a new form of understanding, one which he, as an artist, was capable of imagining. Not, indeed, that he ever had total confidence in his ability. It was not as though he had a hidden blue-print of the plan he was devising. Like most great artists he had to feel his way towards that technique which would allow him to do justice to each moment and each part of his artistic odyssey as it occurred.

In a letter to Stanislaus in 1906 he says: '. . . if I put a bucket into my own soul's well, sexual department, I draw up Griffith's and Ibsen's and Skeffington's and Bernard Vaughan's and St Aloysius' and Shelley's and Renan's water along with my own. And I am going to do that in my novel (inter alia) and plank the bucket down before the shades and substances above mentioned to see how they like it: and if they don't like it I can't help them. I am nauseated by their lying drivel about pure men and pure women and spiritual love forever: blatant lying in the face of the truth'.[49]

His letters to Nora 'display traces of fetishism, anality, paranoia, and masochism' but '[t]hen too, the letters rebuke such obvious labels by an ulterior purpose; besides the immediate physical goal, Joyce wishes to anatomize and reconstitute and crystallize the emotion of love'. 'He likes to boast of his prudishness with men, at whose dirty stories he never even smiles, to give a greater secretive value to his outspokenness with her, and to indicate that this erotic singleness must prove the essential innocence of his nature'. 'They must share in shame, shamelessness, and unashamedness'.[50]

49 *Selected Joyce Letters*, edited by Richard Ellmann, New York, 1975, p. 129.
50 *Ibid.* p xxv.

The attempt to locate Joyce himself in all of this becomes even more difficult when, for instance, we are faced with the much quoted paradox that he was supposed to have told Frank Budgen that everything in *A Portrait of the Artist as a Young Man* was autobiographical whereas Stanislaus maintained that his brother was a creative artist and that, therefore, this and his other works were fictional. In fact both these statements are true in their own way. All the material which Joyce uses is more or less based upon the material furnished him in his own life. One of the exceptional aspects of his make-up was a phenomenal memory. However, this does not mean that his works are slavish recordings of his own life history. On the contrary, the use he made of this autobiographical material was free from any such preoccupation. His creative project was not to record but to express himself and to effectuate the exorcism which would allow him to grow towards the fulfilment which the text prefigures. In other words, 'Joyce is the writer who is writing the text so that the text will produce the writer who can write the text'.[51]

In his famous essay on *Ulysses*, Valery Larbaud claims that the title of *A Portrait of the Artist as a Young Man* 'indicates that it is also, in a certain sense, the story of the youth of the artist in general, that is to say of anyone gifted with an artistic temperament'.[52] This does not seem to be the case. Although the name Stephen Dedalus is symbolic this does not make it universal. The book is a portrait of the artist, the unique artist who was able to produce *Ulysses*. It is of interest to note that *Ulysses* was originally meant to be another story in *Dubliners*. However, the much more extended work that it later became is both the result and the recording of the exorcism which *A Portrait*

51   Colin McCabe, *James Joyce & the Revolution of the Word*, London, MacMillan, 1978, Pp 28-29.
52   'Le titre nous indique que c'est aussi, en un certain sens, l'histoire de la jeunesse de l'artiste en general, c'est-à-dire de tout homme doué du temperament artiste' Valery Larbaud, 'James Joyce', *La Nouvelle Revue Francaise*, nouv. ser., 9e année, 16, no 103, Avril 1922.

achieved in Joyce. The central character of *A Portrait* becomes one point in a triangle in *Ulysses*, each of these points being a different coagulation of colour on the James Joyce spectrum.

The first three episodes of *Ulysses* could be a continuation of *A Portrait*. But then comes the real Odyssey for both writer and reader. Each episode from here on in *Ulysses* is apportioned a specific part of the body as its presiding organism except the first three which deal specifically with Stephen. The real paralysis of Stephen Dedalus, the artist, is not one which is imposed upon him by his surroundings. It is his disembodiment. He is a disconnected spirit. The attempt to make of him a poet is doomed to failure because there is nothing creative in him at all. The matrix of creation is absent. He wanders through the world as a ghostly soul that cannot adhere to anything and cannot, from the inside, release itself from itself.

There is an ironic retrospective glance at the artistic pretensions of Stephen in *A Portrait*: 'Fabulous artificer, the hawklike man. You flew. Whereto? Newhaven-Dieppe, steerage passenger. Paris and back. Lapwing. Icarus. Pater, ait. Seabedabbled, fallen, weltering. Lapwing you are. Lapwing he'.[53] The Stephen who, on the last page of *A Portrait* goes 'to encounter for the millionth time the reality of experience and to forge in the smithy of my soul the uncreated conscience of my race', has become aware of his own impotence. The lapwing is a forger or faker, a bird who leads you away from its nest by bluffing and leading you on.

The last line of *A Portrait*: 'Old father, old artificer, stand by me now and ever in good stead' has failed to happen. In *Ulysses* Stephen has become identified with both the father (Dedalus) and the son (Icarus). He is the father of his own labyrinth and, like the Cretan Daedalus, after whom he is named, he was confined in his own tortuous labyrinth and was unable to escape. The original Daedalus es-

---

53   *Ulysses*, 1958, p. 199.

caped when a natural-born son of his came from outside the labyrinth and released him. Stephen of *Ulysses* is searching for a father who will launch him like Icarus into flight.

There is no question of Joyce identifying with Stephen in his views on aesthetics and creativity as presented in this first part of Ulysses. Joyce is presenting Stephen as the Sabellian-Idealist artist who can only be freed from his paralysing cocoon by the process of the novel itself. It is the novel which holds the secret formula of paternity and not any of the personages within it.

After the first three episodes, without presiding bodily organ, we leave Stephen and enter the world of Bloom. These episodes introducing Stephen's opposite number are presided over by one bodily organ for each of the five: the kidney, the genitals, the heart, the lungs and the oesophagus. The next time we meet Stephen is in the ninth episode.

This ninth episode, Scylla and Charybdis, takes place in the library in which the famous discussion about Shakespeare's *Hamlet* occurs. This is the last episode in which we meet the Stephen of *A Portrait*. Now that we have entered into the body of the novel proper, each episode being presided over by some bodily organ, the brain is the one chosen for this episode. Materially, it deals almost entirely with Shakespearian criticism and is peopled by a group of very thinly disguised Dublin literati of the time. It records a long Platonic dialogue on the personality of Hamlet and the creative presence of Shakespeare in this play, between Stephen Dedalus, Mr Best, John Eglinton, George Russell (AE) and Quakerlyster (the librarian). It includes some lyrics, a short passage in blank verse and another in dramatic form, thus encompassing the three forms of literature defined by Stephen in *A Portrait of the Artist as a Young Man*. However, all this is the decoy of the lapwing luring us away from the real significance of the episode which, as the title of the novel suggests, concerns the odyssey of the twentieth century Ulysses, Leopold Bloom.

In the original odyssey of the mythological Ulysses, the hero had to choose between one of two perilous routes on his way back to Ithaca. He was advised by Circe not to attempt the passage through the 'wandering rocks' but to take the less dangerous of the two, which was the journey between the sheer steadfast rock of Scylla and the whirlpool of Charybdis.

In Joyce's version of the odyssey these two dangers are symbolically present: 'the beautiful ineffectual dreamer who comes to grief against hard facts'.[54] The rock of Dogma, of Aristotle and of Shakespeare's Stratford, is contrasted with the whirlpool of Mysticism, Platonism and the London of Shakespeare's time. The real action of the novel in this episode is the almost breathless passing through of Ulysses. 'A man passed out between them, bowing, greeting'.[55] Bloom, as the twentieth century Ulysses, passes out from the dark gloom of the library into a 'shattering daylight of no thoughts'.[56] His actual presence in this episode takes up no more than a few throwaway lines. But each time this presence is felt, it builds up the real significance of the novel itself.

Just as the moment when the solipsistic Stephen, influenced by both Berkeleyan Idealism and Sabellian modalism is propounding a theory of art and literature which is totally dependent on the author and which leaves absolutely no leeway to the causality of chance, the novel takes over and language disrupts the flow of the episode:[57]

> – Bosh! Stephen said rudely. A man of genius makes no mistakes. His errors are volitional and are the portals of discovery. Portals of discovery opened to let in the quaker librarian, soft-creakfooted, bald, eared and assiduous.

....
54   Ibid. p 172
55   Ibid. p 206
56   Ibid. p 203
57   Ibid p 179.

This chance external event heralds the later arrival of Bloom through these same portals of discovery, disrupting Stephen's attempt to compromise the movement of the novel, the odyssey proper.

However, the most important dislocation of the narrative in this episode occurs when we discover that Stephen's whole theory of and reflections on Shakespeare are a red herring. What he is describing is not Shakespeare at all but the real father figure of the novel, Leopold Bloom. During the episode we are examining, the narrative moves into the internal discourse of Stephen's mind. He is musing about Shakespeare and concocting an image of the latter which is remarkably similar to the character of Leopold Bloom, the father figure for whom Stephen is unconsciously searching. Both Shakespeare and Bloom 'are "overborne" by women, and are forced to marry by the impending arrival of a girl child'. Both lack the self-confidence to win at romance, are ineffective with distant 'Dark Ladies', both stop mating after the second labours of their wives and lose a son after eleven units of time to be left both fatherless and sonless. Both are cuckolds who do not seek redress though they are preoccupied with the brutes their wives take: they return home despite suffering to achieve contentment. And both are avaricious, incestuous and Jewish, qualities Stephen links together.[58] Stephen says to himself on this occasion, 'He was chosen, it seems to me. If others have their will Ann hath a way. By cock, she was to blame. She put the comether on him, sweet and twenty-six. The greyeyed goddess who bends over the boy Adonis, stooping to conquer, as prologue to the swelling act, is a boldfaced Stratford wench who tumbles in a cornfield a lover younger than herself'.[59] This description corresponds to the key scene of Bloom's courtship with Molly on Howth Hill in which she 'got him to propose' and in which Bloom was 'ravished' by her.[60]

---

58   Sheldon R. Brivic, *Joyce between Freud and Jung*, NUP, New York, 1980, p. 136.
59   Ibid. p 137
60   Ibid.

Later in a similar interior monologue, Stephen uses the following very unusual words and images to describe Shakespeare: 'In a rosery of Fetter Lane of Gerard, herbalist, he walks greyedauburn. An azured harebell like her veins. Lids of Juno's eyes, violets. He walks. One life is all. One body. Do. But do'.[61] Now this is all taking place inside Stephen's discourse. But, just to show that the correspondence between Shakespeare and Bloom is not the over-zealous interpretation of the reader, the novel itself makes this connection by repeating, this time, within the very different discourse of the interior monologue of Bloom himself, exactly the same words and also in connection with Shakespeare. In the Sirens episode, Bloom is musing about Shakespeare: 'Music hath charms Shakespeare said. Quotations every day of the year. To be or not to be. Wisdom while you wait'. And immediately after this reference to Shakespeare, he repeats Stephen's words almost verbatim: 'In Gerard's rosery of Fetter lane he walks, greyedauburn. One life is all. One body. Do. But do'.[62]

It is not a question of identifying Joyce with either Stephen or Bloom. 'Joyce creates Stephen and Bloom, juxtaposes them and defines their positions as widely and rigorously separated in order to dramatize a conflict within himself and within humanity which he is unable to reconcile'.[63]

The word made flesh was Joyce's ambition as a writer. How could he transubstantiate himself into a word? This is one of the many reasons why the Roman Catholic Mass should appear in *Ulysses*. Joyce himself would have been brought up with this ritual as a central focus. All the Roman Catholic characters in his novels about Ireland would have had this archetypal structure embedded in their psyche. There are some who claim that along with the Odyssey which serves as the history and memory of the European race, told again through

61   Ulysses p 266.
62   *Ulysses*, p 190.
63   Sheldon R. Brivic, *Joyce between Freud and Jung*, NUP, New York, 1980, p. 165.

the characters of Stephen Dedalus (Telemachus), Leopold Bloom (Odysseus), and Marion Tweedy Bloom (Penelope), in Dublin, Ireland, on June 16, 1904, there is a parallel structure to be found 'in the Offertory, Holy Sacrifice, and Communion of the Catholic Mass, in Roman Catholic Dublin'.[64] Joyce begins the parody of the Mass with Prayers Foot of the Altar, comes to a climax with the Consecration, and ends with the Last Gospel. These coincide with the beginning, climax, and end of the novel. Buck Milligan here is clearly making fun of the priest by carrying his shaving bowl, with crossed mirror and razor on top, as the priest used to carry a Chalice, covered with a crossed veil and burse, when approaching the Altar. The Kyrie in *Ulysses* comes in the Aeolus episode, chapter seven. In the Scylla and Charybdis episode the Gloria follows a parody of the Credo. Joyce's 'black mass' comes at the climax of the novel in the Circe episode of chapter fifteen, at the high point of the brothel scene.

Throughout the novel every form of eating and drinking is compared to a Eucharistic celebration. The drinking of cocoa marks symbolically the finding of the son by the father, the attainment of identification for both, and the human communion. Cocoa is the form whereby the liquid that is Stephen and the solid that is Bloom are contained, and to which Molly [the third person] is symbolically added as 'the viscous cream ordinarily reserved ... for Marion'. The trinity of mankind is now consubstantially complete because of Epp's massproduct, (product of the Mass), the creature cocoa and the added cream. The text has all the pedantic precision of a ritual.

Again as Bloom crosses O'Connell Bridge in episode eight, The Lestrygonians, (Daniel O'Connell being the great emancipator, the instigator of Catholic Emancipation in Ireland), gulls swoop down on Bloom looking for food: 'Looking down he saw flapping strongly, wheeling between the gaunt grey walls, gulls... They wheeled low-

---

64   Briand, Paul L. Jr., "The Catholic Mass in James Joyce's *Ulysses*," *James Joyce Quarterly*, vol. 5, no. 4 (Summer 1968), pp. 312-322.

er. Looking for grub. Wait. He threw down among them a crumpled paper ball... the ball bobbed unheeded... Not such damned fools...' He had crumpled up the piece of paper with his advertisements on it – wafer thin propaganda parading as bread – but the gulls were not to be gulled. So, he buys them real food and scatters it to the wind: 'Wait. Those poor birds... He halted again and bought from the applewoman two Banbury cakes for a penny and broke the brittle paste and threw its fragments down into the Liffey. See that? The gulls swooped silently two, then all, from their heights, pouncing on prey. Gone. Every morsel'. Banbury cakes are flat oval-shaped puff pastries with a filling made in Oxfordshire in England, to secret recipes since 1586. This is real substance scattered to the whole world. 'They never expected that. Manna'. They expected the wafer thin hosts with the advertising propaganda refusing it to the majority, reserving it for the pure.

Great play is made of the two prayers in the vernacular prescribed by Pope Leo XIII in 1884 and 1886 and renewed by Pope Pius X in 1903 to be said after Mass.[65] These appear verbatim at the end of the Lotus Eaters episode, where Bloom is sitting in on a Mass at All Hallows, and in scurrilous parody at various moments throughout the text of *Ulysses*.[66] The Last Gospel always served as a coda for every Catholic

---

65 Let us pray.
    O God, our refuge and our strength, look down with mercy upon the people who cry to Thee; and by the intercession of the glorious and immaculate Virgin Mary, Mother of God, of Saint Joseph her spouse, of the blessed Apostles Peter and Paul, and of all the saints, in Thy mercy and goodness hear our prayers for the conversion of sinners, and for the liberty and exaltation of the Holy Mother the Church. Through the same Christ Our Lord. Amen.

    Saint Michael the Archangel, defend us in battle; be our protection against the wickedness and snares of the devil. May God rebuke him, we humbly pray: and do thou, O Prince of the heavenly host, by the power of God, thrust into hell satan and all the evil spirits who prowl about the world seeking the ruin of souls. Amen.

66 'O, Lust, our refuge and our strength... through yerd our lord, Amen' ['yerd' is a term for 'penis'] is an example from Episode 14, Oxen of the Sun.

Mass: a recapitulation of Catholic belief. In like manner, the interior monologue of Molly Bloom, the Penelope episode, chapter eighteen, acts as recapitulation of the entire novel. Molly's breathless soliloquy is the last gospel of mankind, an affirmation of belief in humanity that begins with yes, is sprinkled throughout with yes, and ends with yes. Molly, to paraphrase in a condensation of St John, is 'the word that was in the beginning and the word that was made flesh'. She is the symbol of flesh, the earth-mother, the everlasting female, the eternal she. Joyce's original intention, according to Ellmann, was to make the Penelope episode into a series of letters from Molly. The ease with which he wrote the episode in the summer and autumn of 1921 was possibly owing to the delivery in March of Nora's obscene letters of 1909 which he had kept hidden in a sealed briefcase. He had written to Ettore Schmitz in Italian (5 January, 1921):

The Circe episode was finished some time ago. The Eumeus episode, which is almost finished, will alsoi be ready around the end of the month. According to plan, Ulysses will appear there [New York] around 15 June next. Now for the important matter: I shall soon have used up the notes I brought with me here so as to write these two episodes. There is in Trieste in the quarter of my brother-in-law in the building bearing the political and registry number 2 of Via Sanita and located precisely on the third floor of the said building in the bedroom presently occupied by my brother, in the rear of the building in question, facing the brothels of public insecurity, an oilcloth briefcase fastened with a rubber band having the colour of a nun's belly and with approximate dimensions of 95 cm. by 70 cm. In this briefcase I have lodged the written symbols of the languid sparks which flashed at times across my soul. The gross weight without tare is estimated at 4.78 kilograms. Having urgent need of these notes for the last incident in my literary work entitled Ulysses or 'His Whore of a Mother', I address this petition to you, most honourable colleague, begging you to let me know if any member of your family intends to come to Paris in the near future, in which case I should be most grateful if the above-mentioned person would have the kindness to bring me the briefcase specified on the back of this sheet.

So, dear Signor Schmitz, if there is someone in your family who is travelling this way, he would do me a great favour by bringing me this bundle, which is not at all heavy since, you understand, it is full of papers which I have written carefully with a pen and at times with a bleistiff when I had no pen. But be careful not to break the rubber band because then the papers will fall into disorder. The best thing would be to take a suitcase which can be locked with a key so nobody can open it.

It seems from this letter, and Brenda Maddox has built a convincing case to this effect, that the 'notes' for which he has an 'urgent need' in order to compose 'the last incident in my literary work entitled *Ulysses*', are indeed the scatological correspondence between himself and Nora which are 'the written symbols of the languid sparks which flashed at times across my soul'.[67] 'Do you notice', he had written to Stannie [9 October 1906], 'how women when they write disregard stops and capital letters'.[68] And to Frank Budgen (10 December, 1920): 'I am going to leave the last word with Molly Bloom – the final episode Penelope being written through her thoughts and body, Poldy being then asleep'.[69] And again (16 August, 1921):[70]

---

67 Brenda Maddox, Nora, *A Biography of Nora Joyce*, London, Minerva, 1989.
68 Ellmann, *Selected Joyce Letters*, op. cit., p. 116.
69 Ibid. p 274.
70 Ibid p. 285

Penelope is the clou of the book. The first sentence contains 2,500 words. There are eight sentences in the episode. It begins and ends with the female word *yes*. It turns like the huge earth ball slowly surely and evenly round and round spinning, its four cardinal points being the female breasts, arse, womb and cunt expressed by the words *because, bottom* (in all senses bottom button, bottom of the class, bottom of the sea, bottom of his heart), *woman, yes*. Though probably more obscene than any preceding episode it seems to me to be perfectly sane full amoral fertilisable untrustworthy engaging shrewd limited prudent indifferent *Weib. Ich bin der Fleisch der stets bejaht.*

This last sentence ['I am the flesh that always denies'] is a reversal of Goethe's Faust who says: 'I am the spirit that always denies'.

The letters hold a secret key just as ALP's letter in *Finnegans Wake* tells the hidden truth about HCE and cryptogrammatically about the world in which we live. The world created by the Word is a conglomeration of 96 elements. The Wake created by Joyce is a conglomerate of words which are combinations of 26 letters. Both these kaleidoscopes of world and Wake can be jostled towards readable configuration if we find the appropriate viewing-point, adjust the focus, and discover the key. The epitome of *Finnegans Wake* is a teastained letter about a woman who is a river, a man who is a city.

Ulysses is a stepping-stone towards something else. As early as 1927 Joyce began to lose interest in it. '*Ulysses!*', he once remarked to Maria Jolas, 'Who wrote it? I've forgotten it'.[71] Even Nora was aware of how relatively unimportant *Ulysses* was when compared with *Finnegans Wake* for a real understanding of her husband's artistic project. After his death she was distressed by the disregard for his last work and said to Maria Jolas: 'What's all this talk about *Ulysses*?

---

71   Richard Ellmann, *James Joyce*, 1983 op. cit., p. 590.

Finnegans Wake is the important book. When are you and Eugene going to write about it?'[72]

However, to understand the true significance of Joyce's last work, which was not a novel, it is important to understand the internal conflict which he used the novel form to exorcise in *Ulysses*. Here Sheldon Brivic, who situates *Joyce between Freud and Jung*, gives an interesting interpretation. He claims that, at the heart of *Ulysses* is a distinction similar to the one which Jung was making in his *Psychological Types* which was written at about the same time (1921). The two types are incarnated in Stephen and Bloom and the whole structure of the novel, especially the Scylla and Charybdis episode, is based upon the distinction between body and soul, matter and spirit. For Joyce the sexual dimension is fundamental and defines the being of a character and, at this level, either excessive materialism or excessive spirituality is destructive. 'Stephen's addiction to prostitutes is a mode of sex without love which ultimately contrasts to Bloom's love without sex'.[73] It implies that Stephen really loathes and denigrates women while Bloom adores and deifies them.[74] Prostitution is an appropriate mode of sex for those who reject the world and devalue their bodies, which explains why the brothel scenes are cluttered with religious imagery.

Freud explains that the wilful cuckold, [Bloom] is really trying to recreate in his wife the original way in which he related to his mother, with the necessary competitor playing the part of the father. This means that Bloom is at the opposite pole from Stephen and is making a God out of woman and, in this way, putting her in the place of the father. These two aspects of Joyce's life are certainly present in his letters and they represent two dimensions of puritanical religious

....

72   Ibid p 743.
73   Sheldon R. Brivic, *Joyce between Freud and Jung*, NUP, New York, 1980, p. 148.
74   Ibid. p 141.

upbringing and highly developed sexual instinct, which for many people create a particularly 'Catholic' temperament.

Brivic's theory is certainly well documented and it is interesting to note that the following commentary by Stanislaus on *Finnegans Wake* would seem to support such an interpretation:[75]

> In the Tyrone Street episode, for instance, the relation or at least the analogy between the imagination in the intellect and the sexual instinct in the body ... is worked out with a fantastic horror of which I know no equal in literature, painting or music ... It is undoubtedly Catholic in temperament. This brooding over the lower order of natural facts, this re-evocation and exaggeration of detail by detail and the spiritual dejection which accompanies them are purely in the spirit of the confessional. Your temperament, like Catholic morality, is predominantly sexual.

At this second level with which we are dealing, the movement of the novel is generated towards the meeting of these two opposites and their returning home together to Ithaca where they are both confronted by the third term of the triangle, Penelope, the earth mother, the Gea Tellus. This movement causes the dislocation of the narrative proper and explains why when Stephen's words turn up in Bloom's monologues or vice versa, 'this isn't a "dropping out of character" but a deliberate dropping of character into some other continuum'.[76] It is this 'other continuum' of Joyce's novels which we must now pursue to the third level of the analysis of Joyce as novelist.

If Joyce cannot be identified with any of his characters and if the revolution of the word was achieved by abstaining from any privileged or dominating discourse on the part of the author, to liberate

75   Richard Ellmann, *James Joyce*, 1983 op. cit., p. 578.
76   Sheldon R. Brivic, *Joyce between Freud and Jung*, NUP, New York, 1980, p. 171.

the text and the reader, what hope is there of establishing the exact relationship which did exist between Joyce as novelist and his novels as texts?

Brivic, in an article called 'Joyce and the Metaphysics of Creation',[77] claims that, although Joyce rebelled against the idea of God in his youth, he later came to realise that he himself must act as God in relation to his creative works and project himself into them as a similarly transcendent principle. All the violations of established styles and dislocations of narrative discourse which have been outlined in the last two sections are, according to Brivic, 'spiritual manifestations, positive acts Joyce performs as God and these miraculous events in the text are productive of one of Joyce's major kinds of reality'. In other words, the destruction of the novel which Joyce achieved in *Ulysses* was not merely a negative reaction of further disenchantment but was the positive creation of another level of reality beyond the confines of the novel and one which would be again recuperated within a text in his last work.

The mental lives of Stephen and Bloom arch towards each other like flying buttresses in the cathedral of *Ulysses*. In the centre is suspended the totality of Joyce constituted by the combination of their two extremes, the sides of his mind that could never be reconciled. Joyce's first entelechy, his personality, is the principle that regulates the relation between parts in his work, and it is only by seeing his living being in all its depth and complexity that we can understand the organization of his world and the tonality of his voices.[78]

Brivic would seem to be nearer to the truth when he quotes the work of Jung[79] than when he derives Joyce's creative approach from a study of Aristotle. Whatever can be said about enlarging the notion

77   Sheldon Brivic, 'Joyce and the Metaphysics of Creation', *The Crane Bag*, Vol. 6, No. 1, 1982.
78   Ibid.
79   C.G. Jung, *The Collected Works*, Vol. 8, Bollingen Series XX, New York, 1960, pp. 419-531.

of causality by reintroducing the disabused 'final' and 'efficient' causes of Aristotelian metaphysics, it seems to me that Joyce's concern was with an a-causal principle of creativity.

In an interview with Beckett in 1957, Ellmann gleaned the following interpretation of Joyce's interest in this regard. 'Joyce's fictional method does not presume that the artist has any supernatural power, but that he has an insight into the methods and motivations of the universe ... To Joyce reality was a paradigm, an illustration of a possibly unstatable rule. Yet perhaps the rule can be surmised. It is not a perception of order or of love; more humble than either of these, it is a perception of coincidence'.[80] This would correspond almost exactly with Jung's description of a similar preoccupation. In his paper on 'Synchronicity: an A-causal connecting principle' he defines this term as 'the parallelism of time and meaning between psychic and psychophysical events, which scientific knowledge so far has been unable to reduce to a common principle. The term explains nothing, it simply formulates the occurrence of meaningful coincidences which, in themselves, are chance happenings, but are so improbable that we must assume them to be based on some kind of principle, or on some property of the empirical world. No reciprocal causal connection can be shown to obtain between parallel events, which is just what gives them their chance character. The only recognizable and demonstrable link between them is a common meaning, or equivalence'.[81]

At this third level of Joyce as novelist, it could be seen, for example, that the Scylla and Charybdis episode of Ulysses, which comes under the organ of the brain, is constantly being lowered from the surface level of narrative causality (and all causality is the idiomatic language of the brain) to another level of synchronicity which introduces a dimension outside the space, time and causality of the

---

80   Richard Ellmann, *James Joyce*, 1983 op. cit., p. 562.
81   C.G. Jung, *The Collected Works*, Vol. 8, Bollingen Series XX, New York, 1960, p. 531.

narrative as such. This echoes the thought of Jung in his essay on synchronicity: 'We must ask ourselves whether there is some other nervous substrate in us, apart from the cerebrum, that can think and perceive, or whether the psychic processes that go on in us during loss of consciousness are synchronistic phenomena, i.e. events that have no causal connection with organic processes'. After a lengthy argument he comes to the conclusion 'that a nervous substrate like the sympathetic system, which is absolutely different from the cere-brospinal system in point of origin and function can evidently produce thoughts and perceptions just as easily as the latter'.

If this third dimension is present in *Ulysses* it is only so as product and not as a total presence. This is why the novel form could not satisfy Joyce. The dimension hinted at in *Ulysses* had to be expressed in a much more positive and immediate way, as presence rather than absence. This takes place in *Finnegans Wake* where Joyce does not content himself with producing the effects of synchronicity within the time-space continuum of a novel but actually works his way back to the a-causal dimension and expresses it directly.

In his essay, Jung shows what a difficult task such a project is: 'The idea of synchronicity with its inherent quality of meaning produces a picture of the world so irrepresentable as to be completely baffling'. The dimension from which such communication must occur is no longer the 'day-time' of *Ulysses* but, rather, what Jung refers to as 'a twilight state'. In such a situation, Jung wonders whether 'the normal state of unconsciousness in sleep, and the potentially conscious dreams it contains, … are produced not so much by the activity of the sleeping cortex, as by the unsleeping sympathetic system, and are therefore of a transcerebral nature'. Such expression would require 'a new conceptual language – a "neutral language" and a modality without a cause which Jung calls a-causal orderedness'. All of which seems appropriate as a description of Joyce's project in *Finnegans Wake*.

Joyce himself is essentially the conflict between certain external pressures and certain internal qualities, which at the particular time in which he lived and with the exceptional gifts with which he was endowed, rose to such a pitch that something had to give way. What eventually did give way was the ground on which both the protagonists were standing. Joyce was forced to find within himself a new dimension, a new reality, for which he then became the channel through his enigmatic last work. Joyce is essentially a provincial poet who was driven by the encroaching limitations of his particular province, or rather city, to dig down to its foundation until he released both it and himself from its narrow confines and connected both to the mainstream of humanity as a universal phenomenon.

The pressures which generated such a violent implosion in this unusually gifted man were many and varied. If any one of the accidental details of his particular biographical circumstances had been absent it might have relieved the pressure to the extent that it might never have reached breaking-point. The important thing for an understanding of Joyce is to see what led to that breaking-point and to what that breaking-point led.

In the first case, there are a number of, sometimes, trivial factors, none of which, on their own, could amount to very much, but which as an accumulation within the structure of this particular psyche were sufficient to ignite the gun-powder. The first of these was Joyce's Catholicity. The second his middle-class background. This is an important addition to his Catholicity because Catholicism was taken more literally and scrupulously by the middle classes than by peasantry or aristocracy. It also means that he had none of the prejudices and awe of tradition and convention with which the 'upper' classes of his day (those who would normally have received as extended an education as he received) might have been encased. These might also have stifled intellectual originality, revolutionary ideology, or interest in the obscene. Mahaffy the famous provost of Trinity

College, Dublin, described Joyce as 'a living argument in favour of my contention that it was a mistake to establish a separate university for the aborigines of this island – for the corner-boys who spit into the Liffey'.[82]

The third pressurizing element was his precocious and predominant sexuality. This might not have become so poignant and so fanatical if it had not been nurtured, or perhaps poisoned, in the atmosphere generated by the first two pressurizing elements. The fourth element was a combination of his exceptional intelligence and the education and cultural formation he was able to achieve. The fifth would be his artistic gifts and temperament, which gave him the strength and patience to withstand such pressures, and the imaginative ability to escape from the labyrinth. The sixth is what I have already referred to as the *Zeitgeist*: he had the good fortune to live at a time when a whole direction of thought was piercing through the confines of the workaday world as it had been understood and defined for centuries. The great psychological discovery of his century was the night world, though he frowned upon the use of that world as a means of therapy, he received from it support and direction in the pursuit of his own originality.

All of these pressures impinging upon a lesser person would have crushed them. Joyce was able to withstand this pressure and convert it into creative energy for two reasons: the first was his capacity for extraordinary artistic self-expression, the second was his fortuitous and symbiotic relationship with Nora. Any understanding of Joyce must attempt to situate the presence of this woman in his world.

So, what did all these internal and external pressures produce in the mind of James Joyce and what did he, in turn produce from them?

The overall impression is of disconnection between the opposite poles of his make-up and a capacity to behave, under different cir-

....

82   Ellmann, *James Joyce* (1983) op. cit., p. 58 n.

cumstances, in a way that seems as opposite as Jekyll and Hyde. The most spiritual and lofty aspirations coincide with the most carnal and obscene thoughts and actions. The Jesuit Joyce and the seducer Stephen abide under the same roof. The one is petulant and almost prudish about other people using foul language or obscenities in his presence, the other is secretly writing letters to his 'whorish wife Nora' which are among the most scatological in the history of letter writing. Then, at a certain point in his life, this schizophrenia melts away. The obscene passion dies out of him to such an extent that Lionel Trilling in his study of Joyce's letters suggests that although 'the substance of the marital correspondence at forty is not different from that of the twenties' there is a change in the quality of Joyce's passion and that this 'devolution from his early egotism of the world to the later egotism of nullity is a biographical event that asks for explanation'.[83] Trilling is so intent upon his cultural theory that Joyce was the man who killed the nineteenth century and, like Sampson, had to kill himself in the process, that he forces upon us the conclusion that 'the letters of the years of fame were written by a being who had departed this life as it is generally known ... and has passed from temporal existence into nullity, but still has a burden of energy to discharge, a destiny still to be worked out'.[84] Trilling sees the 'controlling tendency of Joyce's genius' as a progress which moves 'through the fullest realization of the human, the all-too-human, to that which transcends and denies the human'.[85] I would agree with much of what Trilling says but not the conclusion he reaches.

It is true that the real genius of Joyce was to move 'through the fullest realization of the human, the all-too-human' which he expressed in *Ulysses* to that which transcends 'this life as it is generally known'. But that does not mean that he 'denied' the human or that

83   Lionel Trilling','James Joyce in his Letters', *Commentary*, February,1968, pp.57-58.
84   Ibid.
85   Ibid.

he 'passed from temporal existence into nullity'. It means, rather, that he redefined the limits of humanity and extended temporal existence into another dimension.

Jung was probably the first to call Joyce a prophet.[86] 'There are', he says, 'major and minor prophets, and history will decide to which of them Joyce belongs. Like every true prophet, the artist is the unwitting mouth-piece of the psychic secrets of his time, and is often as unconscious as a sleep-walker. He supposes that it is he who speaks, but the spirit of the age is his prompter, and whatever this spirit says is proved true by its effects'. The other controversial statement which Jung made about Joyce was that, like Picasso, he was schizophrenic. This second remark caused such a furore that Jung had to explain himself in 1934 in a footnote: 'By this I do not mean ... a diagnosis of the mental illness schizophrenia ... but a disposition or habitus on the basis of which a serious psychological disturbance could produce schizophrenia. Hence I regard neither Picasso nor Joyce as psychotics'.[87] The two statements are connected and, in Joyce's case, the schizophrenic gave birth to the prophet. The etymology of schizophrenia describes a cleavage of the mind and a disconnection between thoughts, feelings and actions. That Joyce was temperamentally prone to this reaction is probably best illustrated by the fact that his daughter, Lucia, was, in fact, diagnosed on May 29, 1931, as suffering from hebephrenic psychosis which is a form of schizophrenia characterized by hallucinations, absurd delusions, silly mannerisms, and other kinds of deterioration.

Joyce refused to accept that there was anything really wrong with his daughter, declaring that if she were insane then so was he. However, his attitude towards medicine and psychoanalysis changed radically when he was faced with the spectacle of his demented daughter.

86   C.J. Jung, 'Ulysses: a Monologue', *The Collected Works*, Bollingen XX, New York, 1966, Vol. 15, pp. 122-123.
87   Ibid, p. 137, note 3.

He even agreed to put her under the care of Jung and came to realise that the night-world which he himself was exploring was probably too harsh for ordinary mortals and that the therapeutic and scientific approaches to it, which he had once disdained, were perhaps the only means of access to it for the majority of people. It is interesting to note that the copy of *Ulysses* which was in Jung's library is signed in 1934: 'To Dr. C.G. Jung, with grateful appreciation of his aid and counsel. James Joyce'. Lucia had been under the care of Jung for three months, from 28 September of that same year, when Joyce wrote this dedication. However, Jung was the twentieth doctor to have been consulted and Joyce again refused to accept his verdict and took Lucia back to Paris with him. As a result of this episode, Jung wrote his considered opinion of the two in a letter to Patricia Hutchins:[88]

> If you know anything of my Anima theory, Joyce and his daughter are a classical example of it. She was definitely his 'femme inspiratrice', which explains his obstinate reluctance to have her certified. His own Anima, i.e. unconscious psyche, was so solidly identified with her, that to have her certified would have been as much as an admission that he himself had a latent psychosis. It is therefore understandable that he could not give in. His 'psychological' style is definitely schizophrenic, with the difference, however, that the ordinary patient cannot help himself talking and thinking in such a way, while Joyce willed it and moreover developed it with all his creative forces, which incidentally explains why he himself did not go over the border. But his daughter did, because she was no genius like her father, but merely a victim of her disease. In any other time of the past Joyce's work would never have reached the printer, but in our blessed XXth century it is a message, though not yet understood.

88   Ellmann, *James Joyce* (1983) op. cit., p. 679.

Joyce believed that Lucia was a clairvoyante, that her ravings were similar to his language in *Finnegans Wake*, all of which is important as an approach to this work.

Joyce's schizophrenic temperament drove his several antagonistic aspects to the furthest limits of his personality, thus forcing him to be a completely different person on different occasions. The obvious example is to be found in his letters. Here, as he says himself, 'Some of it is ugly, obscene and bestial, some of it is pure and holy and spiritual' but he adds most significantly, 'all of it is myself'. The cultural and other pressures exercised upon Joyce from his early youth forced him into such a psychic situation – the different parts of him which made up the 'all' of himself were scattered and diversified. Nora was the only person he ever met in his life whom he trusted fully. This meant that he was able to display before her all the most obscene impulses which had been driven to the frontiers and turned into perversions of their real meaning by the overbearing ethos of the time.

The discovery of the 'night world' in the beginning of the century was such an upheaval for most people that it automatically translated itself into their psychological categories in terms of schizophrenia. This world had to be mapped out as a world 'under' or 'over' our own as a 'sub'conscious or 'sur'realist sphere, to which there could be no direct access. This world had to be approached indirectly through the mechanical processes of medicine and science (eg. the interpretation of dreams, which was tantamount to placing two interpreters, one from the underworld and one from our own upper one between the 'patients' and the other side of themselves). This world, like the face of Medusa the gorgon, could not be looked at directly, but could only be sighted indirectly through a mirror forged in our technological world.

Joyce as prophet became the direct mouthpiece for such a dislocated reality. Whether by disease or natural genius he was able to situate himself in a psychic dimension, which is for others as yet only available in such unconscious states as sleep, and retain his consciousness sufficiently to allow expression of this dimension to filter through into a text. Jung calls this 'visceral thinking' (in which case he points to the presiding bodily organs in each episode of Ulysses as significant) or 'conversation in and with one's own intestines' which describes a process 'of almost universal "restratification" of modern man, who is in the process of shaking off a world that has become obsolete'.[89]

The whole perspective which governs our world in terms of latitude and longitude, outer and inner, conscious and unconscious, past, present and future, dream and reality, is one which was fashioned by humankind as spectator to the universe instead of participator in the universe. The particular gifts of Joyce allowed him to situate himself quite 'naturally' at another place within himself, from which place the language of *Finnegans Wake* flows. Joyce was not 'consciously' trying to be perverse and to write in a way that was deliberately exotic. He said to John Eglinton about the language in *Finnegans Wake*, 'I write in that way because it comes naturally to me to do so'.[90] Writing at this level, and from this level, participates in the real motive force of the universe. It does not just describe the observed causality of the universe, it participates in the psychic dimension of that a-causal connecting principle which is the real motor force of the world. Jung quotes Sir James Jeans as saying that it is possible 'that the springs of events in this substratum include our own mental activities, so that the future course of events may depend in part on these mental activities'.[91]

This would mean that Joyce was a prophet in the very real sense of having tapped the resources of a language which did not content

89 C.J. Jung, op. cit., Vol. 8, Pp. 119; 513.
90 Ellmann, *James Joyce* (1983) op. cit., p. 546.
91 C.J. Jung, op. cit., Vol. 8, p. 513.

itself merely with describing the causality of the world from a distant and observational point of view, but which actively enmeshed itself in the well-springs of such causality. That Joyce, himself, was aware of such a possibility is suggested by his remark to Oscar Schwarz in Trieste, 'My art is not a mirror held up to nature. Nature mirrors my art' and his claim that there were many examples in his work of clair-voyance where future events had borne out predictions carried in his earlier work. This would mean that Joyce had discovered a language the resources and power of which have not, as yet, been imagined.

The teleological genius of Joyce allowed him not to be dislocat-ed and dispersed among the schizophrenic elements of his make-up but to creatively pursue these energies to another apex where they achieved a unity of being which opened up for him and for us a new dimension of humanity, a new definition of the 'I', as Hermon Broch wrote in 1949, 'an "I" that is at once the *sum* and the *cogito*, at once the logos and life, reunited; a simultaneity in whose unity may be seen the glow of the religious per se' and in which we can sense 'the germ of a new religious organization of humanity'.[92]

Finnegans Wake is directly connected to the reality it describes in the same way that the dream is indistinguishable from the world of the unconscious to which it gives expression. Here language is not the translation of a reality into a text, it is the immediate textual gesture of that reality itself. The work of the author of such a text is not that of establishing the causal connection between one word and the next, as if words were cut and dried atoms with a quantified quota of univocal sense. Here the author's job is to find within each word the peculiar gesture of itself which will reveal an unsuspected and hidden reality which will, quite by accident, lead on to the next unforeseen gesture of language. 'For you may be as practical as is predicable' Shem says of his use of language in *Finnegans Wake*, 'but

----

92   Herman Broch, 'Joyce and the Present Age', *Yearbook, 1949*, pp. 106-107.

you must have the proper sort of accident to meet that kind of being with a difference'.[93] This describes the artistic process of *Finnegans Wake*. It is the unconscious as language itself, not the unconscious described by language. The text itself is woven out of the hidden energy sparked off by language whose entirely fortuitous gestures, under the guiding hand of the author, provide a providential similarity of sound or appearance in a word, thus revealing new connections between two or more beings indicated by that word.

Early on in the Wake, Joyce advises us to stop if we are 'abced-minded'.[94] Here the use of language is not as an ABC of signals which refer to concepts in a shorthand morse code. Language in the Wake is a series of gestures of being and the work of the author is to search for the 'nameform that whets the wits that convey contacts that sweeten sensation that drives desire that adheres to attachment that dogs death that bitches birth that entails the ensuance of existentiality. But with a rush out of his navel reaching the reredos of Ramasbatham'.[95] This is not the language of the mind, it is visceral language that rushes out of the intestines from a nervous substrate like the sympathetic system, which is quite different from the cerebrospinal system which produces the rational language of ordinary discourse. Language at this level, as a gesture of being, is nearest to, on the one hand, the scatological language of Joyce's letters, used to procure a directly physical effect and, on the other, to the eschatological language of the sacramental tradition in which Joyce was reared, through whose efficacy was achieved the perfect reality of the thing signified. It was through the powerful medium of such language that Joyce achieved the final unification of these two otherwise contradictory opposite sides of himself. *Finnegans Wake*, far from being the final discharge of energy of a being who had transcended the limits

---

93   *Finnegans Wake*, Faber, 1975, paperback edition, p. 269.
94   Ibid. p 84.
95   Ibid. p 18

of the 'all-too human' and arrived at the non-human void of nullity, described by Lionel Trilling, is the discovery of language as that gesture of being which establishes a new dimension of humanity from which these two supposedly antagonistic principles of the spirit and the flesh can achieve a hypostatic union in the person of a new kind of creative writer.

An interesting parallel, which may help to explain Joyce's use of language in *Finnegans Wake*, can be drawn between his use of words and the use of paint by an artist like Francis Bacon. Bacon says that 'the texture of a painting seems to come immediately onto the nervous system'[96] that 'the mystery of fact is conveyed by an image being made out of non-rational marks ... that there is a coagulation of non-representational marks which have led to making up this very great image'. The way he works is by making 'involuntary marks on the canvas which may suggest much deeper ways by which you can trap the fact that you are obsessed by'.[97] Both these artists are aware of an a-causal principle, which they call chance or accident, which is the ultimate source of their work. As Bacon puts it, 'One knows that by some accidental brushmarks suddenly appearance comes in with such vividness that no accepted way of doing it would have brought about. I'm always trying through chance or accident to find a way by which appearance can be there but remade out of other shapes ... To me the mystery of painting today is how can appearance be made. I know it can be illustrated, I know it can be photographed. But how can this thing be made so that you catch the mystery of appearance within the mystery of making?'[98]

These descriptions of Bacon's use of paint in accidental brushmarks seem to describe the similar task which Joyce set himself in words in his 'work in progress'. Language in this work takes on itself

....

96   David Sylvester, *Interviews with Francis Bacon*, London, 1975, p. 58.
97   Ibid. p 53
98   Ibid. p 105

a role which it has never before been allowed to fulfil. It is given the freedom and the power to speak the meaning of the humanity which for so long held it in a subservient role of polite and obedient servant. Like the role of the butler in Barrie's play *The Admirable Crichton*, it becomes the most important character in a situation where the lords and ladies of civilized society find themselves shipwrecked on a desert island. In the new situation, which the accidental course of history imposes upon human society, a new priesthood is necessary to provide the words of salvation which will satisfactorily cope with the life-style which has been forced upon us. The discovery of the 'night-world' of the unconscious at the beginning of the twentieth century represents such a shipwreck of the values, the philosophy, the world-view of Western civilization.

Finnegans Wake is an attempt to actuate a new being adequate to the situation, by allowing language to dig up the letter from the dump-heap of the world. A kind of ritualistic or ceremonial attitude towards language is required: 'The ring man in the rong shop but the rite words by the rote order!'[99]

Just as Joyce was prevented from becoming a poet by the education he received and the culture which surrounded him, so the twentieth century is incapable of creating its own meaning until it takes seriously the real source of its possible resurrection: the mystery of the 'root language' which holds 'the keys of me heart'.[100] *Finnegans Wake* is European civilisation represented by the mythic figure (Finn), who has died, restored to a new life (again) but this time a(wake) conscious one, through the regenerative power of language. In this work: 'Yet is no body present here which was not before. Only is order othered. Nought is nulled. Fuitfiat!'[101] The Latin words bespeak the re-creation and resurrection of contemporary mankind,

---

99 FW 167.
100 FW 626.
101 FW 613.

HCE (Here Comes Everybody), who is in the process of shaking off a world that has now become obsolete.

For what was the Western world except a projection of the human mind as both these realities were understood. Now language comes as a tidal wave from the unconscious, not something 'out there' and available for use, like an overcoat or a briefcase, but like an everflowing river that runs through us and through all the ages of our history. The river will, if we listen to it, whisper to us the secret of our origins, while at the same time it will wash away the architecture of a world built without adverting to it. The artist of language in this capacity is the guardian and shepherd of being as it expresses itself through the traces of all recorded human utterance, the anatomy of language:[102]

> ...when the call comes, he shall produce nichthemerically from his unheavenly body a no uncertain quantity of obscene matter... with this double dye brought to blood heat, gallic acid on ore, through the bowels of his misery, ...the first till last alshemist wrote over every square inch of the only foolscap available, his own body, till by its corrosive sublimation one continuous present tense integument slowly unfolded all marryvoising moodmoulded cyclewheeling history ...

The artist 'reflecting from his own individual person life unlivable' creates a text 'transaccidentated through the slow fires of consciousness' which is 'perilous, potent' and 'common to allflesh'.[103]Language here becomes 'the squidself which he had squirtscreened from the crystalline world' of the subconscious, a history of man's unconscious life.

Part I vii of *Finnegans Wake*, where Joyce gives a portrait of himself as Shem the Penman and provides an apologia for his use of language

---

102 FW 185-6.
103 FW 613.

in the Wake, describes the new kind of thinking which is language as the principle of paternity.

In this section there is a retrospective account of all Joyce's writings up to *Finnegans Wake*: *A Portrait of the Artist* is described as a 'wetbed confession', all the stories in Dubliners are denigratingly mentioned by name,[104] and Ulysses is described as a forgery.[105] This renunciation of his style of writing in the past as 'pseudostylic shamiana ... piously forged palimpsests slipped in the first place by this morbid process from his pelagiarist pen',[106] is a prelude to the description of his new kind of writing in *Finnegans Wake*. 'In writing of the night', he says in a letter, 'I really could not, I felt I could not, use words in their ordinary relations and connections. Used that way they do not express how things are in the night, in the different stages – conscious, the semi-conscious, then unconscious. I found that it could not be done with words in the ordinary relations and connections'. *Finnegans Wake* is written 'to suit the esthetic of the dream, where the forms prolong and multiply themselves, where the visions pass from the trivial to the apocalyptic, where the brain uses the roots of vocables to make others from them which will be capable of naming its phantasms, its allegories, its allusions'.[107]

This attempt to express the 'dark night of the soul' was 'a long, very long, a dark, very dark, an allburt unend, scarce endurable, and we could add mostly quite various and somewhat stumbletumbling night'.[108] In this 'Jungfraud's Messongebook'[109] we are never quite sure whether the language is 'd'anglas landadge or are you sprakin sea

104 FW 186-7
105 '. . . what do you think Vulgariano did but study with stolen fruit how cutely to copy all their various styles of signature so as one day to utter an epical forged cheque on the public for his own private profit...' FW 181.
106 FW 181-2'.
107 FW 546.
108 FW 598
109 FW 460

Djoytsch?'[110] Here '[t]he war is in words and the wood is the world'.[111] Joyce struggles with language to twist it into shapes ('Imeffible tries at speech unasyllabled') and to crush it into forms ('quashed quotatoes'[112]) so that '[t]he silent cock shall crow at last'[113] and a hidden silent world oozes into speech.

Such a use of language allows Joyce to '[p]sing a psalm of psexpeans, apocryphul of rhyme!'[114] which exploits every aspect of the syllables which compose the words. 'Yet to concentrate solely on the literal sense or even the psychological content of any document to the sore neglect of the enveloping facts themselves circumstantiating it is just as hurtful to sound sense...'[115] This is not a scientific use of language which would translate into clear-cut and unambiguous terms. It is a surpassing of the principle of non-contradiction by a supralogical use of words, each one containing at least 'two thinks at a time'.[116] The pun, in Tindall's phrase, is mightier than the word because it uses the referential medium of sound to spark off correspondences simultaneously tangential to those suggested by the shapes. The artist of such a language does not fly in a cerebral fashion over the forest of language, he situates himself in the thick of the jungle and hacks away at the roots of vocables until he reaches that 'root language' which holds 'the keys of me heart'.[117]

The difference between Stephen and Shem is in their attitude to, and their use of language. Both are 'self-exiled in upon his ego' and 'writing the mystery of himself in furniture'. But Shem has found the way out of the solipistic cocoon back beyond the confines of his own consciousness. He has learnt to produce 'nichtthemerically' (a word

110 FW 485
111 FW 98
112 FW 183
113 FW 473
114 FW 242
115 FW 109
116 FW 583
117 FW 626

that combines the ideas of 'night-time', 'nonthematic' and 'numerically') 'from his unheavenly body' what Stephen is trying to unfold thematically from his heavenly body, disconnected from the material world.

It is the same Joyce who creates the two protagonists. As he says himself: 'Yet is no body present here which was not there before. Only is order othered'.[118] The order of being has been othered by the installation of language in the paternal role. Language is the main character in *Finnegans Wake*. Starting with the very particular European city of Dublin and the particular life of an individual author, the generative power of language leads the artist into an underworld of the universal unconscious, much as the entry into any particular subway station will lead down to that network of underground correspondences which connect with every other one.

The Wake of this universal dimension requires the sleep of ordinary language and the daytime logic of the cerebrospinal cortex.

This new kind of poetry which is *Finnegans Wake* is a recreation of the myth of European man. It provides a restratification of the order of values as these had been developed at every level from philosophy to art. It introduces a new principle of a-causal orderedness through which art participates in the essentially synchronistic pattern of coincidence which Joyce understood to be the movement of life. But most important of all, it accomplished a revolution in the field of ethics, both at a personal level for Joyce himself, and at a universal level for all those who come after him. This ethical adventure was nothing less than the creation of a new alphabet of the heart which sought to join heaven and earth, the body with all its urges and imperfections and the soul, sexuality and sanctity. Not being a string of pearls it strove to be a rosary of opals. It could not be accomplished in his own mind alone. He had to find a partner whom he could trust utterly.

....
118 FW 613

This person had to be someone to whom he could pour out his heart unreservedly right down to the very dregs, without fear of misunderstanding or rejection. And this was achieved to a shocking level, as anyone who reads his letters will discover to their discomfort. There has been an almost tabloid notoriety attached to the publication of the so-called 'dirty' and 'pornographic' letters of Joyce to his wife. These were published by Richard Ellmann in *Selected Letters of James Joyce* which appeared in 1975. The letters had been discovered after the 1966 publication in three volumes of Joyce's correspondence.[119] It is understandable that the couple's grandson, Stephen, should have been affronted by the breach of privacy involved. These letters, in his view, were intimate, private, personal correspondence, never intended for public viewing, which were pirated and sold in an intolerable and shameless invasion of privacy. He published his disapproval in a letter to the editor of the *International Herald Tribune* (10 July, 1984) where he names and blames Richard Ellmann and Nelly, the wife of Stanislaus Joyce. Whatever about these reservations, the letters are now in the public domain and form part of the mystery which it is our business to unravel. In the introduction to *The Selected Letters* which contain the controversial correspondence in unexpurgated form, Richard Ellmann claims:

> Frank as these letters are, their psychology can easily be misunderstood. They were intended to accomplish sexual gratification in him and inspire the same in her, and at moments they fasten intently on peculiarities of sexual behaviour, some of which might technically be called perverse. They display traces of fetishism, anality, paranoia and masochism but [t]hen too, the letters rebuke such obvious labels by an ulterior purpose;

---

119 *The Letters of James Joyce*, Vol. I, II, III, ed. Stuart Gilbert et alia, The Viking Press, 1967.

besides the immediate physical goal, Joyce wishes to anato-mize and reconstitute and crystallize the emotion of love.[120]

You know now how to give me a cockstand. Tell me the small-est things about yourself so long as they are obscene and se-cret and filthy. Write nothing else. Let every sentence be full of dirty immodest words and sounds. They are all lovely to hear and to see on paper even but the dirtiest are the most beautiful. The two parts of your body which do dirty things are the love-liest to me. I prefer your arse, darling, to your bubbies because it does such a dirty thing. I love your cunt not so much because it is the part I block but because it does another dirty thing. I could lie frigging all day looking at the divine word you wrote and at the thing you said you would do with your tongue. I wish I could hear your lips spluttering those heavenly exciting filthy words, see your mouth making dirty sounds and noises, feel your body wriggling under me, hear and smell the dirty fat girlish farts going pop pop out of your pretty bare girlish bum and fuck fuck fuck fuck my naughty little hot fuckbird's cunt for ever.

I am happy now, because my little whore tells me she wants me to roger her arseways and wants me to fuck her mouth and wants to unbutton me and pull out my mickey and suck it off like a teat. More and dirtier than this she wants to do, my lit-tle naked fucker, my naughty wriggling little frigger, my sweet dirty little farter.

Write more and dirtier, darling. Tickle your little cockey while you write to make you say worse and worse. Write the dirty words big and underline them and kiss them and hold them for a moment to your sweet hot cunt, darling, and also pull up your dress a moment and hold them under your dear little

120 Ellmann, *Selected Joyce Letters*, op. cit., p xxv.

farting bum. Do more if you wish and send the letter then to me, my darling brown-arsed fuckbird.[121]

The change which Lionel Trilling detects in Joyce from his earlier to his later correspondence with Nora is the result of his confessions to her and his transformation of the stuff of his deepest yearning into the creative word of his artistic work. Although 'the substance of the marital correspondence at forty is not different from that of the twenties' there is a change in the quality of Joyce's passion and this 'devolution from his early egotism of the world to the later egotism of nullity is a biographical event that asks for explanation'.[122] The explanation for this transformation of the scatology of the early letters is the eschatology of *Finnegans Wake*. The correspondence between Joyce and Nora Barnacle is a clearance of the Augean stables. She was his spiritual guide, sharing with him the deepest levels of their wholehearted humanity. To reach the foundation beneath this grim reality, as Richard Ellmann suggests, 'they must share in shame, shamelessness, and unashamedness'.[123] What happened between them at the level of private correspondence over a hundred years ago should take place today, at the level of public national consciousness, if we are to benefit from this artist's intuition and become his contemporaries.

If we are to achieve access to our inner world, so that this inner world in all its depth and darkness can be excavated and charted, we need to engage in this dialogue with our intestines, with the most private recesses of our humanity. Joyce became the mouthpiece for such a dislocated reality. Whether by disease or genius he was able to situate himself in such a psychic dimension and filter this into a text. Jung calls this 'visceral thinking' or 'conversation in and with one's own intestines'. He describes this as nothing less than a 'restratifi-

---

121 Letter of 9th December, 1909, Ellmann, *Selected Joyce Letters*, op. cit., p. 186.
122 Lionel Trilling, 'James Joyce in his Letters', *Commentary*, February 1968, pp. 57-8.
123 Ellmann, *Selected Joyce Letters*, op. cit., p xxv.

cation' of contemporary humanity 'in the process of shaking off a world that has become obsolete'.[124] The 'stomach language' of this 'prepronominal funferal, engraved and retouched and edgewiped and puddenpadded, very like a whale's egg farced with pemmican' makes no easy reading. Each sentence has to be 'nuzzled over a full trillion times forever and a night till his noddle sink or swim ... by that ideal reader suffering from an ideal insomnia'[125] who has to forget the way he was taught to read, and allow language to become the 'aural eyeness'[126] which will provide the 'keys to dreamland'.[127]

The image which Joyce uses to describe the source and the production of this new language is the sepia ink secreted by a squid. The house of Shem the Penman is described as 'the Haunted Inkbottle', wherein 'this double dye' is 'brought to blood heat through the bowels of his misery'. Just as the ink of an octopus is part of its being, so language is 'the squidself which he had squirtscreened from the crystalline world'; it is not a translation, it is the reality itself. It comes from his reflecting upon 'his own individual life unlivable' and his processing of the various 'scalds and burns and blisters, impetiginous sores and pustules' through 'the slow fires of consciousness'. Its effect is not just an individualistic web of the artist's own making, a predictable, orderly and impotent ego trip. This language creates 'a dividual chaos, perilous, potent, common to allflesh'.

The element in it which creates this escape route is its 'antimonian manganese limolitmious nature', whose 'corrosive sublimation' works itself back through the artist's individual consciousness until it reaches 'one continuous present tense integument' which slowly unfolds 'all marryvoising moodmoulded cyclewheeling history'.[128]

---

124 C.G. Jung, *The Collected Works*, Vol. 8, Bollingen Series XX, New York, 1960, p. 513;119.
125 FW 120
126 FW 623
127 FW 615
128 FW 184-9

It is in this sense that language, as the generating third term in the triangles of literature and psychology, becomes the father for whom Joyce was searching. As a corrosive river it can journey back into the deep recesses of the psyche to provide a meeting-place for those antagonistic principles which manifested a conscious state of schizophrenia. In terms of literature, it objectifies a 'general omnibus character', inclusive of all the elements of 'homogenius' humanity, in the shape of a new kind of father-figure, 'the Great Sommbody within the Omniboss'[129] or 'someone imparticular who will somewherise for the whole'.[130]

The 'some where' which will summarise the whole of 'cycle-wheeling history' is the city of Dublin. The 'general omnibus character' who personifies this totality of manhood is the Earwicker family. Although there seem to be several members of the family and several variations of each member, each one characterises one aspect of the integrated human omnibus. It is also difficult to distinguish them from the topography of the 'anywhere' of Dublin. H.C.E., the original father-figure, is identified with the hill of Howth, Chapelizod and Phoenix Park. He is the masculine principle whose initials spell out his universality in their variation as 'Here Comes Everybody'. His wife A.L.P., identified with the river Liffey which runs through the city, is the feminine principle, 'annyma' (anima), called Anna Livia Plurabelle. His daughter Issy is-a-belle who can represent any and every kind of girl, while his sons, Shem and Shaun, are those familiar, age-old, warring twins, equal and opposite, who inhabit each one of us in varying combinations. They are the rivals who compose the banks (*rivae*) of the river.

The structure within which their family history is unfolded is provided by Vico and Bruno. The coincidence that Dublin does have a Vico road which 'goes round and round to meet where terms be-

---

129 FW 415
130 FW 602

gin',[131] and a bookshop called Browne and Nolan, act as proof of the universal principle which Joyce understood to be a paradigm of reality. Both literature and life were one 'grand continuum, overlorded by fate and interlarded with accidence'.[132]

Language, as an alluvial deposit, is both the source and the texture of this grand continuum. 'In the buginning is the woid'[133] is Joyce's variation on the opening to St John's Gospel. Language, as father, replaces the monarchical autonomous principle by an anarchical and heteronomous one. The void of the word (woid) is constitutive of language. Although a 'thing-of-words', language is not a 'thing-in-it-self' because words, however autonomous they may appear, are always referential, their being is to relate to something else. Language is the fluid principle of continuity between the 'squidself' of the artist-father and the 'squirtscreened' image of his consubstantial son at every level of creation from theology to literature. Far from being an invention of human consciousness to act as mere communication, language is an aboriginal source of meaning which flows through history and humanity, by whose shores the artist, as an alert and zealous beachcomber, is called to read 'the signature of all things'.

The text of *Finnegans Wake* is an artistic creation of this reality on paper: 'For that (the rapt one warns) is what papyr is meed of, made of, hides and hints and misses in prints'[134] which does not mean that it is a 'riot of blots and blurs' although it 'looks as like it as damn it',[135] for it is the work, as Joyce says of himself, of 'one of the greatest engineers if not the greatest in the world'.[136] When it was finished he wrote to Miss Weaver: 'I have passed 24 hours prostrate more than the priests on Good Friday. I think I have done what I wanted to do'.[137]

131 FW 452
132 FW 472
133 FW 378
134 FW 20
135 FW FW 118
136 Ellmann, *Selected Joyce Letters*, op. cit., p. 321
137 Ibid.

CHAPTER THREE

○

Murdoch as Mentor

Iris Murdoch's life as a series of facts is simple enough: born in Dublin in 1919 as only child of a happily married couple, she grew up and was educated in London and studied at Oxford. She worked as a civil servant during World War II and returned to Oxford in 1948 to teach philosophy. She wrote 26 novels, some plays, a book of poems and three philosophical treatises. She married John Bayley in 1956 and became a Dame of the British Empire in 1987. She died from Alzheimer's disease at the age of 80.

Peter J. Conradi in his 2001 biography fills in the surrounding shades and tones in over 600 pages, most of which are devoted to her very extraordinary love life. This is where many readers may have been shocked, some because they had imagined her as a virgin, others because they hadn't known what was going on! If there are criticisms to be made of this painstakingly scrupulous account, they would be, in my view, the relentless accumulation of undifferentiated detail and the eventual attempt to 'explain' her amorous odyssey in terms of Conradi's own Buddhist world-view: 'She wanted Buddhism to educate Christianity, to create a non-supernatural religion'.[1]

Thomas Aquinas divides the moral life into two categories: those who obey rules and are protected by laws and those whose whole lives are put at risk in the cause of morality. Iris Murdoch's life and work were an intimately intertwined spiritual journey. The novels she wrote [24 in all] can be read as cardiographs of her artistically transmuted experience of the realities she courageously explored

---

1   Peter J. Conradi, *Iris Murdoch, A Life*, HarperCollins, London, 2001, p 597.

about human beings in love. Her life was, in this sense, morally heroic and pioneering. As a woman she dared to philosophize with her whole being and invented the art form capable of carrying that wisdom. Love was one of the schools of transcendence, a laboratory of life, where 'goodness', she believed, could be distilled.

She had at her disposal a restricted social and geographical sample of humanity, but with this sample she underwent the full gamut of relational possibility. She was amazingly liberated and courageous for the times she lived in, and relentlessly determined in her exploration. Like Jane Austen who created her novels from 'three or four families in a country village' where she found 'human nature in the midland counties', Iris Murdoch found human nature in the friends who surrounded her, mostly at Oxford. Her novels describe her journey with accuracy and acuity. They must be one of the most perspicacious accounts of human intimacy ever recorded.

Nor was her journey easy for her. She was by nature and upbringing a puritan and a prude. But she saw it as her task to be both Ariadne and Theseus to the twentieth century that she loved so much. 'I get a *frisson* of joy to think that I am of *this* age, *this* Europe – saved or damned with it' she says in a letter of 6 November 1945. Virtue is sometimes the courage to do whatever is necessary to release ourselves from bonds of slavery. For one person it may be the very opposite to what is required for another. Too many have identified it with one particular manifestation. We have sometimes called virtue the incapacity to accede to any virtue whatsoever.

'I should tell you', she writes to the man who loved her and who died in the war, Frank Thompson, 'that I have parted company with my virginity. This I regard as in every way a good thing. I feel calmer and freer – relieved from something which was obsessing me... I am not just going wild. In spite of a certain amount of wild talk I still live my life with deliberation'. He replied to her reporting his fear that she had been wedded to 'a cold virginity' and 'so, on balance, it is obviously a subject for joy'. She wanted to smash the image of herself that everyone seemed to share: a prim blue-stocking, 'Iris was always virginal' her friends declared. So, she, wanting to reach herself and the century in which she lived, confides: 'I want to hurl myself down into the melee and the mud and I don't care how filthy it is...'

Nor was this simply obstinate contrariness or *la nostalgie de la boue*, it was in the nature of a vocation. But 'it is not what one has experienced but what one *does* with what one has experienced that matters' is another secret of which she was aware. The villain of her century was Hitler; the corresponding villain of her love-life was Elias Canetti.

Iris Murdoch studied at Cambridge and was professor of philosophy at Oxford University for over fifteen years. She read the great philosophers from Plato to Wittgenstein. She seems to have come to the conclusion that philosophy is a game invented and played by men. It is supposed to answer all the fundamental questions about human existence but fails to do so, mostly because it is too cerebral, too abstract, too scientific, too generalised. Her fundamental intuition is that life in its human manifestation is unique, unpredictable, messy. Trying to capture it and freeze-frame its essence, as a butterfly collector might display specimens in a cabinet, is an impossibility. The mystery of human existence is too mercurial and elusive to be trapped in any butterfly net however fine the mesh. 'Human lives are essentially not to be summed up, but to be known, as they are lived, in many curious partial and inarticulate ways'.[2]

In the extract from her unfinished book on Heidegger, she claims that his originality was to highlight the futility of that search in terms of traditional philosophy. '*Dasein* (the German term is used in En-

2   Letter to David Hicks, January, 1943, quoted in Peter J. Conradi, *Iris Murdoch, A Life*, HarperCollins, London, 2001, p 529.

glish translation)[3]... is a sort of relation, or world-awareness, or be-
ing-there of a world.... *Dasein* is (partly, proximally) describable in
terms of its states of mind: moods, anxieties, fears.... Heidegger reasonably claims (178:139) that "the basic ontological interpretation
of the affective life in general has been able to make scarcely one
forward step worthy of mention since Aristotle. On the contrary, af-
fects and feelings come under the theme of psychological phenomena, functioning as a third class of these, usually along with ideation
and volition. They sink to the level of accompanying phenomena."
(And, one might add, become the property of novelists.)[4] Murdoch
pursues this argument on the next page saying that 'a good novelist can more accurately describe these fugitive aspects of the human
condition, but of course that is not philosophy, and the novelist too
has his formal purposes'.[5]

She abandons 'the game' of philosophy and writes novels which
would capture and unfold certain aspects of the human predicament.
Her first, when she was thirty-five in 1954, she called *Under the Net*,
as if to convey the depths into which she had to dive in order to examine the reality which lies below and beyond the nets [a favourite
image of Wittgenstein,][6] as of the hunters and trappers in the history of philosophy who tried for over two centuries, at least in the
Western-European tradition, to stalk and capture this same prey.

Philosophy's advantages and strengths in terms of clarity, precision and muscularity of thought, are the very reasons why it becomes
powerless in the realms of human being. This is not just because the
heart has reasons which reason cannot know, as Pascal has said, but

3   'Heidegger uses the term Dasein, 'being there', to indicate, in the most general
     and initially vague sense, human awareness, consciousness, something there.
     Dasein is also primordially Being-in-the-World. It is its world'. Iris Murdoch, *Sein
     und Zeit*: Pursuit of Being, in *Iris Murdoch, Philosopher, A Collection of Essays* edited
     by Justin Broackes, Oxford University Press, 2012, p 95.
4   Ibid. p 96.
5   Ibid. p 98.
6   Wittgenstein's *Tractatus*, 6, 341, for instance.

because our understanding is wider than the narrow compass of our reasoning. Such knowing is quite other than the form of epistemology which we have learnt from modern science, which never begins from what we don't know to lead us towards what we might conjecture from experience. On the contrary, most epistemologies begin from what we do know, and do know with absolute certainty, to build a sure and certain system which explains our universe.

Iris Murdoch took her sample of humanity from the elite and articulate group who happened to be with her at Oxford at a particular time in its history and in hers. The fact that the world of her novels is a limited and privileged one does not preclude the possibility of commenting upon the moral nature of human being in general. 'Criticism of novels on the basis of class is very silly and very artificial', Murdoch scolds Stephen Glover who accuses her of writing 'bourgeois novels'. 'Why should one have to write about the working class to write about reality? One can only write about the world one understands. What one deeply knows about, at least in my case, is fairly limited. [But] these are the sort of people I know. It's very difficult to... jump out of your class. I write about human nature'.[7] Human nature is everywhere the same no matter into which historical era, social class, ethnic identity or geographical region it may happen to be inserted. The imperative for the novelist is to write about what they know. Oxford in the twentieth century is as good a place as any to find human nature in the raw, and perhaps a better place than most to engage the reality of this nature, because the sample at one's disposal is likely to be more aware and more articulate.

Iris Murdoch, as moral philosopher, anthropologist and explorer, used [questioning like Socrates] her social set in Oxford as a laboratory wherein she undertook the alchemy of her art. She lived and

7   Interview with Stephen Glover, 1976, *From a Tiny Corner in the House of Fiction*, Conversations with Iris Murdoch, Ed. Gillian Dooley, University of South Carolina, 2003, Pp 40-42.

used the interpersonal relationships which were woven between herself and her friends in and around the university of Oxford, as a paradigmatic love machine which acted as the crucible wherein she experimented, and through which she almost tortured the human condition into confessing to her the secrets of the deepest recesses of the human heart. 'Like Socrates, perhaps', she confides to her journal,[8] 'love is the only subject on which I am really expert?' Harold Bloom ranked her 'only below Proust and Freud as a major student of Eros, an original and endlessly provocative theorist of the tragi-comedy of sexual love'.[9]

In *The Sovereignty of Good*[10] she holds that the central task of the moral agent involves a true and loving perception of another individual, who is seen as a particular reality external to the agent. How does one achieve that goal? Not in any abstract intellectual philosophising, but in hands-on discovery of how it works in day-to-day encounters with people whom we love. Personal relationships are the setting within which this moral activity is accomplished.

> The moral task is not a matter of finding universalizable reasons or principles of action, but of getting oneself to attend to the reality of individual other persons. Such attention requires not allowing one's own needs, biases and desires regarding the other person to get in the way of appreciating his or her own particular needs and situation.[11]

There is a deal of jealous, misogynist bitterness aimed at Iris Murdoch on the part of those highly articulate males who made up the

8   Journal entry, 9 July 1976.
9   Harold Bloom, 'A Comedy of Worldly Salvation', New York Times Book Review, 12 January 1986, pp.30-31, quoted in Peter J. Conradi, *Iris Murdoch, A Life*, HarperCollins, London, 2001, p 595.
10   Iris Murdoch, *The Sovereignty of Good* (London: Routledge and Kegan Paul, 1970).
11   Lawrence A. Blum, Iris Murdoch and the Domain of the Moral, *Philosophical Studies* 50 (1986) 343-367.

ingredients of her novels as studies in moral philosophy. The studied attempt to undermine her status and her role as expert and original contributor to the history of moral philosophy is based upon subjective and often hysterical evidence that her thinking was borrowed or stolen, her personal love life promiscuous and immoral, her novels tawdry and trivial. How could such a slatternly charlatan be taken seriously as a moral philosopher in the line of Aristotle, Spinoza, or Kant?

The answer is that she dedicated her so-called 'immoral' life to the high purpose of exploring the meaning of 'love' and she recorded her journey through this jungle of uncharted territory in the only way that this was possible, in the log-books of those novels which she created [almost one a year] over the quarter of a century which was given to her to undertake such a perilous and heroic task. We, her beneficiaries, have now the possibility of introducing a more enlightened kind of loving into the twenty-first century, with the highly readable and relevant case histories she has left us in her published works.

Peter Conradi writing a closing letter to David Morgan for his book about the love Iris had for him expresses this well:

> Your book also touches on a delicate and interesting question that she repeatedly addressed in her Gifford lectures in my hearing in 1982, but which I think may be missing or under-stated when she came to write these lectures up as *Metaphysics as a Guide to Morals*. She took the view that *even the most virtuous apprehension of another human being need not necessarily exclude an erotic element*. This, I remember her repeating, could quietly co-exist with other elements within a friendship. She believed that this erotic element could be implicit rather than explicit and, if expressed at all, should be so only up to defined limits, one primary duty of the good moral agent being to sublimate 'low Eros'. A difficult feat, one extremely liable to misunderstanding or misrepresentation by outsiders – but

one she had the courage to learn to carry out. And you show this, too [120].[12]

In one of her letters to Morgan, she describes the place she is trying to reach and to preserve as the ultimate source of personhood in her herself and in other people. She is aware that it is a difficult space to salvage but that unless we do so we are likely to be invaded by the being of others and never to achieve our own identity. 'I know how one feels that one person can make one be at last oneself. But there has got to be also a central point, even if it is very small, which knows it can and has got to survive in the face of anything and be indestructible'.[13] Marie-Louise von Franz, the Jungian analyst who was a contemporary of Iris Murdoch, and famous for her interpretation of fairy-tales, has described a similar conviction as 'a feeling of standing on solid ground inside oneself, on a patch of inner eternity which even physical death cannot touch'.[14]

Iris Murdoch transformed the very real stuff of her own extravagant and varied love life into the 'moral' tales which are her legacy, the library of novels which endure. This work was a process quite different from the business of philosophy; it was a process of creation which involved the unconscious as much as the conscious life.

Ethics as 'first philosophy' precedes any 'knowledge' of a formulated kind. Ethics is what encounters the strangeness of the Other, his or her irreducibility to the I, to my thoughts and my possessions, before I ever get time or space to organize my world-view. In the 1960s there were parties in extravagantly liberated circles, or so we hear, where rooms were filled with foam rubber and participants

---

12 David Morgan, *With love and Rage, A Friendship with Iris Murdoch*, Kingston University Press, 2010, p. 120.
13 David Morgan, Ibid. p. 136, which is Letter number 4 from Iris Murdoch to David Morgan, dated 30th June 1965
14 Marie-Louise von Franz, *C.G.Jung, His Myth in our Time*, New York, C.G.Jung Foundation, 1975, p 74. Quoted in Sallie Nichols, op. cit. p 352.

took off all their clothes and insinuated themselves into the mixture so that they could encounter other bodies in a tactile fashion without having to see them as a preliminary. This immediate corporeal intertextuality, as it were, precluded the possibility of *a priori* mental constructs which would prejudice unpremeditated collision with the other as other. 'Metaphysics', or whatever word we want to use for our most comprehensive explanation of ourselves and the world we live in, must be the kind of 'knowledge' which can accommodate such primal connection with the 'Other'; all attempts to understand will eventually reduce this experience to manageable proportions and incorporate it into my internal explanation of my world, unless I take the precautions necessary to preserve essential resistance to all such epistemological monopoly.

The life and work of Iris Murdoch have therefore caused something of a revolution in the area of Ethics as a branch of Philosophy, often referred to as 'moral philosophy'. This used to be something of an applied science wherein the philosopher applied to the area of human behaviour and endeavour, those principles which had already been worked out in the areas of metaphysics and epistemology. Iris Murdoch starts from the other end. She immerses herself totally in the web of human relationships and from her descent into that seething quagmire she filters through her whole being the total experience as this as lived by her from year to year, in the written artistic form of a novel. The total library of her oeuvre spreads a web of understanding and a structure which establishes itself as the pattern of her discourse on love.

Total immersion in the cauldron of human emotion which we have simplistically and generically labelled 'love' is required. Iris Murdoch created such a cauldron out of the charged minefield of relationships she happened to find in the privileged setting she happened to occupy. She more or less compelled all those with whom she was interconnected in that restricted spectrum and space to be guinea-pigs for her experimentation in the area of human morality. This was no detached observer watching and commenting from the heights above; this was a fellow swimmer in the lake of molten lava which is raw humanity in search of love. 'Iris Murdoch's novels are a coruscating analysis of the human capacity to turn love into power-games; the most uncompromising scrutiny of what takes place in the tyrant's cage which masquerades as a happy marriage'.[15]

Epistemologically, therefore, the novel takes over from the philosophical treatise as the most effective method of communicating ethical and, perhaps, metaphysical truth. In a recent book Rowan Williams suggests that 'The human system of knowing cannot be spoken of except as a spiral of self-extending symbolic activity'. In other words epistemology as symbolic expression of lived reality. 'Art is an acute case of knowledge in general', Williams suggests. 'Hence the claims that art has an "ontology" implicit in it. It is not decorative or arbitrary but grounded in what we ought to call a kind of obedience. The artist struggles to let the logic of what is there display itself in the particular concrete matter being worked with. What is involved in knowing is more like re-enacting a performance than labelling an object'.[16]

Each of Iris Murdoch's novels is symbolic performance of what she has elucidated from a lived life. Hence her definition of literature as 'close dangerous play with unconscious forces'.[17] The novel is the language which can cope with a new centre of gravity poised between the conscious and the unconscious. 'A lot of old nightmares have got inside this novel', she says in one of her private journals in June, 1971.[18] These are not just her 'old nightmares', they are nightmares from the century in which she lived. Thanks to her life of explora-

....

15   A.N.Wilson, *Iris Murdoch as I knew her*, Hutchinson, London, 2003, p 6.
16   Rowan Williams, *Grace and Necessity*, Continuum, London, 2005, Pp 137-142.
17   Iris Murdoch, *Existentialists and Mystics*, [hereafter referred to as EM], ed. Peter Conradi, Chatto & Windus, London, 1997, p 195.
18   Peter J. Conradi op.cit. p 522.

tion and penetration, we too can be awoken from such nightmares and shown the path towards more unselfish love. 'We need a moral philosophy in which the concept of love, so rarely mentioned now by philosophers, can once again be made central'. Art is our supreme 'clue to morals'. But, she is fully aware that

> although art can be so good for us, it does contain some of those elements of illusion out of which its detractors make so much of their case. The pierced structure of the art object whereby its senses flow into life is an essential part of its mortal nature. Even at its most exquisite art is incomplete. Art, like (in Plato's view) philosophy, hovers about in the very fine air which we breathe just beyond what has been expressed.[19]

Jane Austen, one of the authors admired by Iris Murdoch, restricted her writing to the very limited and particular society into which she was born. She described her work in the preface to *Northanger Abbey* and *Persuasion* as 'the little bit (two inches wide) of ivory on which I work with so fine a brush, as produces little effect after much labour'. Iris Murdoch might have said, modestly, something similar about her own writing. *From a Tiny Corner in the House of Fiction* is not only one of her frequent descriptions of the great mansion of literature and her place in it, but the title chosen for a collection of 'conversations' with her which took place over the years of her creative and productive life.[20]

Certainly the *Dramatis Personae* of her life and of her novels are a star-studded cast. Heidegger and Wittgenstein share the metaphysical infrastructure. The first she never met personally, the second was one of her teachers. Both had a profound influence on her thinking,

19 EM xiv-xv.
20 *From a Tiny Corner in the House of Fiction*, Conversations with Iris Murdoch, Ed. Gillian Dooley, University of South Carolina, 2003.

as, indeed, they had on the thinking of the century in which they lived. Many of her novels interrogate the 'anxiety of influence' itself. 'Murdoch' George Steiner observes,

> has long been fascinated by the phenomenon of the "coven," of the cult, of the mimetic apprenticeship which has surrounded certain masters of thought (*maîtres à penser*) from Pythagoras and Plato's academy to the time of Wittgenstein... Where Hegel sets Master and Servant at the core of phenomenology, Iris Murdoch places the teacher and the taught, the guru and the adept.[21]

Iris saw Wittgenstein as both numinous and demonic. 'She dreamt of him all her life (never of Sartre), gave *Tractatus* aphorisms to the mystical Nigel in *Bruno's Dream*, and started *Nuns and Soldiers* teasingly: 'Wittgenstein – . "Yes?" said the Count'. Part of what doubtless fascinated her was the way he commandeered his students' lives, humiliated and sometimes excommunicated them...[T]he atmosphere around Wittgenstein was 'emotional and esoteric'; later she spoke of him as evil'.[22] This is all the more strange as Ray Monk in his biography of Wittgenstein quotes Iris as saying 'I only met him twice and didn't know him well and perhaps that's why I always thought of him, as a person, with awe and alarm'. Perhaps she heard about him from some of his students; perhaps she saw in him the same kind of power that she exercised over hers; whatever her source of perception she said of him: 'His extraordinary directness of approach and the absence of any sort of paraphernalia were the things that unnerved people... with most people, you meet them in a framework, and there are certain conventions about how you talk to them and so on. There

---

21 George Steiner in Foreword to Iris Murdoch *Existentialists and Mystics*[EM], Chatto & Windus, London, 1997, p xi.
22 Peter J. Conradi, *Iris Murdoch, A Life*, HarperCollins, London, 2001, p 263.

isn't a naked confrontation of personalities. But Wittgenstein always imposed this confrontation on all his relationships'.[23] Heidegger dominates the later novels especially *The Green Knight*, *The Message to the Planet* and *Jackson's Dilemma*. She spent the last ten years of her life trying to understand Heidegger and write a book about him.[24]

Others in the cast are somewhat less exalted but they include her husband John Bayley, a novelist and literary critic of no mean standing, Elias Canetti, winner of the Nobel Prize for literature in 1981 [a prize which, A.N.Wilson says he had awarded to himself a good half-century earlier],[25] Donald McKinnon, whom George Steiner describes as 'that most searching of modern British moral philosophers',[26] and Franz Baermann Steiner, 'one of the greatest Latin scholars of twentieth century Europe' in A.N.Wilson's view. Franz and her lover who was killed in the war, Frank Thompson, became paradigms for the various scholar-saints in her novels: the good slave in *Acastos*, Saward in *The Flight from the Enchanter*, Willy Kost in *The Nice and the Good*, Tallis Browne in *A Fairly Honourable Defeat*, Ludens in *The Message to the Planet*. An equivalent number of extraordinary women make up the female wardrobe: Elizabeth Bowen, Beryl Bainbridge, Elizabeth Anscombe, Philippa Bosanquet, Margaret Hubbard, whom some of the friends suggest, was the model for Honor Klein, to mention but a few. The game of recognition, as Steiner calls it, is tempting: 'A Sartre, a Canetti, a Donald MacKinnon... declare themselves in the *personae* of the novels as, one ventures to suppose, they did in the author's own biography. Central to Iris Murdoch's imag-

23   Ray Monk, *Ludwig Wittgenstein, The Duty Of Genius*, Vintage, London, 1991, p 498.
24   The first chapter of this book has been published as *Sein und Zeit*: Pursuit of Being, in *Iris Murdoch, Philosopher, A Collection of Essays* edited by Justin Broackes, Oxford University Press, 2012, Pp 93-109. The basis for this publication is the typescript now in the Iris Murdoch archive at Kingston University and the manuscript which is in the Library of the University of Iowa.
25   A.N.Wilson, *Iris Murdoch as I knew her*, Hutchinson, London, 2003, P 87.
26   Foreword to EM p x.

inings are the strangeness, the solitude, the psychological and social risks inherent in the "examined life".[27]

However, we have to resist such temptation and recognise also that the process of writing novels can be compared, using Barbara Pym's homely image, to making chutney. 'You put in the various ingredients, fruit, onions, vinegar, which for some days retain their separateness. Then at some point they turn; they become something different'.[28] Although her friendship with Philippa Foot has been recognised and identified in *The Nice and the Good*, Iris did not meet the model for Anne Cavidge until after the book *Nuns and Soldiers* was written [Marjorie Locke or Sister Ann Teresa who left the Anglican-Augustinian convent of St Mary's Wantage]; whereas no less than four people (two of them women) were offended by the portrait of the old man in *Bruno's Dream* thinking it was based on themselves.[29] Whatever the exact correspondence between the various characters in her novels and the precise personages of her acquaintance, there can be no doubt that her life and her work have been influenced especially by an identifiable group of friends and lovers. A.N.Wilson suggests that as Turgenev was unable to write fiction unless he was mildly in love, Iris Murdoch was unable 'to fire on all cylinders' unless she was 'in love with two objects at once; to be giving her heart to contradictory objects of desire'. He singles out Donald MacKinnon and Elias Canetti as the two 'Prosperos' of her 'formative years' who were 'of supreme importance imaginatively speaking'.[30]

Father figures and mother archetypes work in both directions. A.N.Wilson who says he was asked by Iris to write her biography until he discovered that this job had also been given to Peter Conradi, who happened to do it more speedily and more objectively, also admits

27   Ibid Pp x-xi.
28   A.N.Wilson, *Iris Murdoch as I knew her*, Hutchinson, London, 2003, P 175.
29   The four were Lord David Cecil, BMB [Beatrice May Baker], J.B.Priestly and Elizabeth Bowen as described by Peter J. Conradi, op.cit p 439.
30   A.N.Wilson, *Iris Murdoch as I knew her*, Hutchinson, London, 2003, p 174.

that Iris was a mother figure to him [his first sight of her was when he was about to be nineteen and she was fifty] and that when he went to Oxford she and John Bayley 'were parents to me'.[31] It might not appear like that to those who read *Iris Murdoch as I knew her*, which is Wilson's fulfilment of his biographical commission in spite of its apparent annulment, or at least of its pre-emption by the previous publication of Conradi's approved biography. But, in spite of much that Wilson says, which admirers of hers might deplore and describe as biting the hand that fed him, he does pay her tribute:

> I can only say that in her presence you felt that you were with a person who was not like other people. She was highly intelligent, obviously – but one has met other highly intelligent individuals. It was a quality of depth that you felt. It was an observant depth. And you also felt that, as well as surveying and noticing, IM was looking at that part of her friends' beings or souls of which they were not quite aware themselves. It was the part which could choose to be a good or a bad person. You felt in IM's presence a spiritual power.[32]

This diagnosis of the educational eros which attracted Iris Murdoch to her pupils, and in turn held them in thrall, is similar to what the Greeks named *Paideia*. The term meant 'education of youth' in the broadest sense. Such education was not about learning a trade or an art—which the Greeks regarded as mechanical tasks unworthy of a learned citizen – it was about training for liberty (freedom) and nobility (the beautiful). Oxford was as near to the environment envisaged by Greek culture as was possible to recreate. The Greek mentality was 'to always be pre-eminent'. Homer records that King Peleus set this ideal before his son Achilles, and the ideal can be summed

31 Ibid p 12.
32 Ibid p 37.

up in one word: *arete* in its basic sense, meaning excellence of any kind. '*Arete* was the central ideal of all Greek culture'.[33] Sometimes translated as 'virtue', the word describes 'being the best you can be', or 'reaching your highest human potential'. Ancient Greeks used the word for every eventuality from the breeding of young bulls to the training of nobility. In this latter instance, it is the ability to '*make his hands keep his head* against enemies, monsters, and dangers of all kinds, and to come out victorious'.[34]

This ideal was to be carried out and transmitted by the aristocratic class, who had already embodied and intellectualized it sufficiently to pass it on to their pupils. These are then 'moulded' to the ideal. The root of the word is the same as *aristos*, the word which designates superlative ability and superiority. Adult aristocrats were encouraged to fall in love with the youths they mentored. The *kalos kagathos* ['the beautiful and the good'] was the goal, and this ideal was carried through to the middle ages in the culture of the medieval knights, as it was in the nineteenth century in the concept of 'the gentleman'. Such was the expressed ideal of Iris Murdoch's philosophy.

A poignant example of her attempt to put this into practice has been recorded by David Morgan in his account of their relationship.[35]

Morgan was the ideal version of the young bull who needed to be transformed by Iris into a knight in shining armour. He was born in what he describes as 'the most non – of non-places, a commuter suburb of Birmingham'. He had an interrupted education that included a school for maladjusted boys and he left without qualifications. He educated himself sufficiently to con his way into the Royal College of Art. Theirs was an unlikely love story: she was a successful 44-year-old writer with seven darkly philosophical novels to her name, and a

---

33   Jaeger, *Paideia* I.15.
34   Jaeger, *Paideia* II.56.
35   David Morgan, *With love and Rage, A Friendship with Iris Murdoch*, Kingston University Press, 2010.

critical reputation to match; he was a penniless autodidact who had spent time in a mental asylum, before conning his way into art school on the strength of a hastily scribbled outline of his left foot.

Anne Rowe has a perceptive take on their relationship:

> Embroiling herself in Morgan's life was partly an aspect of Murdoch's own liberation, and partly an attempt to immerse herself in behaviour which she sought to understand and subject to moral questioning in her art... She understood that altruism is often infected with self-seeking, yet she was clearly appropriating Morgan's life for her art.[36]

Morgan also saw her as a mother figure:

> I wouldn't call her maternal, but in this respect she was like a mother – the only other figure we dare do this with. The trouble was that as with a mother, you were driven to test her to the limit to prove to yourself over and over again that you were safe.[37] I am the first to testify that she was one of those rare people whose first instinct when they see anybody in trouble is to put things right. And she tried to put my troubles right over and over again.[38]

> The London Iris of the '60s and '70s was a brave figure who rushed about helping people – listening to them, paying for them, educating them, bucking them up, making them believe in themselves – a figure very much in charge.[39]

---

36 Ibid. p xvii.
37 Ibid. Pp 34-35.
38 Ibid. p 38.
39 Ibid. p 75.

Their relationship was touchingly 'platonic' by more recent standards, but it is certainly true to say that Iris was in love with him. Sometimes the asymmetrical shape of this connection and the two quite different motivations for their mutual attraction are bewildering, but often Morgan's descriptions of Iris are hilarious:

> What did she look like – to me? I found her fierce 'Joan of Arc' look attractive. But I found her body dumpy and, by the time I met her, middle-aged spread had been added to her natural stockiness as a girl. Ungallantly therefore, when she made her ground rules at Harcourt Terrace (You won't be able to go to bed with me) I was at first surprised that it had been brought up at all, then relieved.... What did she wear?... She could vary from aristocratic bag lady to female Cossack with trousers and tunics. My usual impression was of trailing voluminous tweed coats that could have been from Oxfam, but weren't.[40]

A.S. Byatt, whose study of the early Murdoch novels in 1965 was intuitive and influential, claimed that Iris was her 'literary mother'.[41] According to Conradi, Byatt was 'frightened' at their first meeting, and was still alarmed twenty-five years later. We are left with such a wealth of commentary from so-called 'parents' and 'children' of this enigmatic artist that later biographers are forced to create a posthumous pastiche somewhat akin to one of her own novels to piece together the jig-saw created by so many disparate and varying interpretations.

The person who 'saved' her from enslavement to various 'father figures', and especially from her relationship with Elias Canetti, was

---

40 Ibid. p 14.
41 Although Byatt expressed a dislike of this phrase in a letter to Iris Murdoch's official biographer Conradi in 2000, [cf footnote in his biography p 653] she did allow it to be included in the 1994 edition of A.S.Byatt, *Degrees of Freedom*, Vintage, London, p 338.

John Bayley. She referred to him as 'Puss' and described him to her journal as 'a good man'. Both her biographers seem to agree with this assessment. 'If enslaved herself, an improbable rescuer was to hand',[42] Conradi concludes his account of her life before Bayley appeared, and the chapter introducing him is called 'An Ideal Co-Child'.[43] A.N.Wilson begins by telling us that 'JOB was my tutor at New College, and has been a dear friend and mentor and supporter of mine'.[44] He then describes in detail a visit they made together in 1974 to the rooms of medieval history tutor, Eric Christiansen. As they knock lightly and push open the door,

> an extraordinary scene meets our eyes. Eric is lying on the large black leather daybed. Some bright turquoise arms are clutched about him, and a head of hair is tousled against his shoulder. The two figures are not undressed, but they are tightly entwined. Eric gets up very hastily from the daybed and blinkingly puts on his spectacles back on his nose. The turquoise figure stands up. It is I[ris] M[urdoch].[45]

The impression given is that Bayley was a pathetic cuckold who had to stand by and watch [perhaps even enjoy] his wife's sexual exploits with an army of suitors, both male and female.

There may be some truth in this but it is not the whole truth. John Bayley was one of the very few 'good' people in Iris Murdoch's life and her life was an attempt to define the Good and conduct herself in this light. So she was an expert in this area and no person was better qualified to choose the ideal partner with whom she would share her life. They may have been 'Children of the Forest' or 'Babes in the Wood' in the eyes of those around them but the 'happiness' of

42 Peter J. Conradi, *Iris Murdoch, A Life*, HarperCollins, London, 2001, p 374.
43 Idid. Pp 376-406.
44 A.N.Wilson, *Iris Murdoch as I knew her*, Hutchinson, London, 2003, p 27.
45 Ibid. P 175.

their marriage was legendary. 'Marriage provided what generals call a "base for operations." Iris did not want a bourgeois or conventional marriage. This arrangement procured her a child-wife in John, who cooked, assembled picnic meals – *Wind in the Willows* food, she called it in *The Sea, The Sea* – and who would modestly prefer to say that he acted more as "comic relief" to Iris than as a sheet-anchor. His absence of intensity and his common sense alike were a tonic, preventing her other deep friendships from becoming too serious... he acted as Prospero, "a sort of controller of the demons and spirits who flew in and out of her consciousness".[46] It was this 'base for operations' which allowed Iris to set up the laboratory of love which would be her contribution to the understanding of morality. And John was not simply her facilitator; he was an essential partner in this immense undertaking. He and she began to share access to the unconscious which gave rise to the creative writing which both began to deploy. Iris developed a symbiotic relationship with John. 'Love for J. deepening in all sorts of tender and absurd mythologies'.[47]

On a postcard to me, John Bayley described himself as writing the novel *The Red Hat*, 'for Iris', an attempt to extend her spirit, almost as if he were writing the novel in her place. I had written to him the previous August describing how such a collaboration might now be happening and comparing it to W.B. Yeats's writing *A Vision* through the mediumship of his wife, both of them sharing, or having access to the same unconscious 'place' from which the work emerges.

The books John Bayley wrote about Iris before she died and after her death seemed to A.N. Wilson and others

---

46 This is an important observation about the marriage of Iris Murdoch with John Bayley as it comes from the biography of Conradi, of which Bayley approved, and it involves a quotation from her other biographer A.N.Wilson which provides double confirmation of the analysis. Cf Peter J.Conradi Op. Cit p 402.
47 Peter J. Conradi, *Iris Murdoch, A Life*, HarperCollins, London, 2001, p 404.

a Pandora's box of which he quite clearly lost control. The resentments, envy, poisonously strong misogyny and outright hatred of his wife which seemed to me to come from the books, like some ghastly truth-drug, or course of psychotherapy, brought to the surface of the page, were things of which he probably had only a hazy consciousness. To one old friend who expressed her dismay at the books, he admitted that he thought he had gone mad.[48]

His first book. *Iris: A Memoir*, on which the film starring Judi Dench and Jim Broadbent was based,

> is completely compelling, precisely because we feel the narrator to be revealing much more of himself and his own mixture of motives and emotions than he can have appreciated when he sent the typescript to the publisher. He tells us that he feels more physical affection for IM demented than he had done for IM when sane. One has uncomfortable memories... of Hartley being kept a prisoner in *The Sea, The Sea*. Or, again, one remembers *The Queer Captain*, JOB's own Michael Innes-ish thriller, in which a woman is imprisoned in a remote house, rather like Mrs Crean-Smith in *The Unicorn*. The border-lines between love-object and victim, or lover and prison guard, form part of both the Bayleys' published fantasy life.[49]

All of which, it seems to me, only illustrates the unconscious imbroglio which these two people had become as a result of their strange and symbiotic marriage over a period of forty years. Such an intuition is borne out by an equally strange incident recorded by Ralph Steadman, artist in residence at the Cheltenham Literature

---

48 Ibid, p 9.
49 A.N.Wilson, *Iris Murdoch as I knew her*, Hutchinson, London, 2003, p 258-259.

Festival in 1994. Two of his sitters, among others ranging from Alan Bennett to Joanna Trollope, were John Bayley and Iris Murdoch.

> They shuffled in like bewildered refugees. The couple strange-ly merged as one and so I made a triptych of the 'three' of them. Out of the faces of both emerged a dream face, a puck-ish reinvention of an earlier life. The result was immediate yet complex, simple and personal, an abstraction of the essence I must have sensed, or to be completely fanciful, was willed upon me.[50]

One could surmise that it was this 'trio' also which allowed Iris the space and the security to undertake the exploration of morality which is her legacy. The person from whom John Bayley saved Iris and who certainly exercised a determining influence upon her life and her creativity was Elias Canetti.

> Canetti represented the artist-as-manipulative-and-sadis-tic-mythomaniac who had struck a Faustian bargain, the mys-tifier-enchanter Iris feared turning into, whom indeed she might have become. Her assertion that the structure of good literary works is to do with 'erotic mysteries and deep dark struggles between good and evil' owes much to these years... Canetti had done her lasting service. He had shown her to her-self; and something of the corruptible relationship between pity and power.[51]

This is the description given by Peter J. Conradi, Iris Murdoch's 'official' biographer. In a later article he suggests that 'through

---

50   'The Unseen Faces of Iris' appeared, along with this quote from the artist, in *The Guardian*, 10 February 1999.
51   Peter J. Conradi, *Iris Murdoch, A Life*, HarperCollins, London, 2001, p 373-4

Canetti she discovered something about the workings of power, and her own complicity in this'. He suggests that 'many of her best novels have Canetti somewhere behind them' and that he is 'present within or behind every male enchanter-figure' of her novels from *Flight from the Enchanter* and *A Fairly Honourable Defeat* to *The Sea, The Sea*. 'Later power-figures such as Charles Arrowby and Julius King are better-realized than Fox; they help – retrospectively – illuminate Mischa Fox'.[52]

Canetti himself, at the age of eighty penned a portrait of his relationship with Iris which caused dismay in some quarters. His description is important both because of his intimate knowledge of her, and their intense relationship, but also because his analysis reveals a truth about both of them to which only lovers could have access. Rather like one of her own novels, detailed inspection of what he says about Iris Murdoch will tell us more than we are ever likely to find out elsewhere because his obsessive projections reveal a hatred based upon her usurpation of the role and the genius which he had delineated for himself. No one has more clearly explained the precise genius of Iris Murdoch than has Elias Canetti in his ranting diatribe against her for having outplayed him at his own game.

'You could call Iris Murdoch the bubbling Oxford stewpot', he begins.[53] 'Everything I despise about English life is in her. In her time she has been in love with innumerable men (not to mention many women), but they were special men, each of them a specialist in his own chosen field, whom she took up with. There really were all sorts: a theologian, an economist, an ancient historian, a literary critic, an anthropologist, and also a philosopher and a writer.

'The relationship I know most about is the one with the writer, which is me'. The literary critic (and historian) is her husband, John

----

52 Peter J. Conradi, 'Holy Fool and Magus' in *Iris Murdoch, Philosopher, A Collection of Essays* edited by Justin Broackes, Oxford University Press, 2012, p 128.
53 Elias Canetti, *Party in the Blitz*, Harvill Press, London 2005, p 216.

Bayley, with whom she has lived these past forty years... But all these men she has taken into her, they're all metamorphoses of herself. Her characters spring from the endless discussions she's had with all these men. The women are herself, her woman friends and her girl students, but everything comes out of that Oxford air, in which, thanks to her readiness to love, she has moved and remained with astonishing ease.

'...I might say she has made a lot of booty from me, but it is mixed with so much other prey, that I'd feel ashamed: it's really more of a liability... She listens to everything, again and again, as long as people can stand to repeat it, she offers herself in exchange for more, calmly listens to stories, confessions, ideas, despair. She strikes me as being like a housewife on a shopping expedition. She forgets nothing, you live on in her in a light, irresponsible way, because only philosophy is responsible, and ethics. She also takes on board religions, cumulatively, if you like, never out of any despair of her own, she has her suppliers. Simone Weil is quoted with as much respect as Wittgenstein or Plato'.[54] 'She had a buried robber's nature, and her aim was to rob each one of her lovers not of his heart, but more of his mind'.

Murdoch portrayed Canetti in her second published novel, *The Flight from the Enchanter*, as the cunning Mischa Fox, a mystery-man who, being no friend to independent women, tries to seize and destroy a Suffragette newspaper, *The Artemis*. She dedicated the novel to Canetti who resented her depiction of him.[55]

> She also had an astonishing relationship with time. She had divided it all up. To her it was like a teacher's timetable. When she called, she would say she was coming at 3.15, and she would have to leave at 4.15. It... was always... set in advance by her how much time she had free, and even though it was about

54   Ibid.
55   Peter Conradi in *the Guardian* reviewing *Party in the Blitz*, Saturday, July 9th 2005.

what she termed love, never would she have allowed herself to take more than the allotted time for it.[56]

He, on the other hand, 'at that time in England' 'was happy to give my time to absolutely anyone. For thirty years or more, I was lavish, if not wasteful with it, because I never... became enslaved to the clock'.[57] Canetti then reveals in his memoirs that he was consciously looking for people to write about like 'a secret historian' or a 'spy' desiring to become *der Hund meiner Zeit* [the bloodhound of his epoch]

> I, then, was more of a listener than an analyst, and I was given so much to listen to that I could fill hundreds of volumes with it, if I could remember it. Even the portion that I did remember was sufficient for several books, but I wouldn't even think of going to such a source. All I am interested in is having a few people come to life that at that time became characters to me.[58]

Adler suggests that Canetti's 'shrewd eye for sexual constellations and marital relations' produced an 'educated mix' which nonetheless reveals the 'armchair anthropologist familiar with the writings of Margaret Mead and Bronislaw Malinowski'. His real grudge against Iris Murdoch is that she was far more successful at doing what he regarded as his unique gift. 'He turns her into a counter-image of himself', Adler again suggests, 'attacking her with unrestrained ferocity, dismembering every thread of her being... Every word seems to quiver with rage'.[59]

Canetti presents Iris as 'his polar opposite, objectifying his own character in his sketch... It reads in part like a satirical inversion

----

56   Elias Canetti, *Party in the Blitz*, Harvill Press, London 2005, p 222.
57   Ibid p 238.
58   Ibid p 150 and also quoted by Jeremy Adler in the Introduction, Ibid, p 10.
59   Ibid p 39.

of Canetti's own nature'.[60] She was able to parcel out her time, he was a victim of time-consuming predators. These 'sucked my blood because they weren't slow to notice that I am prepared to listen to anyone who bemoans his confusion, and on and on'. What he never learned to do, not even in England, 'was to manage my time'.[61] England for him was a series of 'detailedly insipid conversations'.

> For a lot of people I became a sort of addiction they weren't able to resist. I listened closely for a long time, I was very scrupulous about that always... it was my passion to hear whatever people wanted to tell me... If it didn't sound quite so ridiculous, I should have to say that I was always a spy, a spy who followed all the various types of humanity, and wherever I saw a particular type, then I listened with even greater attention than usual.[62]

Iris was a far more successful spy and was able to do what Canetti was not able to do, convert her pickings into best-selling paperbacks. Her secret was successful management of time and of timetables. 'There are people', he continues, 'for whom such management amounts to a *raison d'être*. It becomes as important, or more important than their dependants, their spouses, even their pets. More than anyone, I was astounded by Iris, who always had a schedule, even for love'.[63]

She used to invite him to Oxford, meet him at the station 'wearing grotesque sandals, which showed off her large flat feet to terrible disadvantage'. He 'could not ignore the ugliness of her feet. She had a bearlike walk, but it was a repulsive bear, crooked and purposeful at once'. She would walk him from the station 'pushing a bicycle with one hand' and stopping at a 'dingy' shop 'to buy some wretched provisions – ends of

60   Ibid p 40.
61   Ibid p 230.
62   Ibid p 152.
63   Ibid p 230.

cheese, bread, not even any olives – for lunch... Anything less hospitable, more dismally puritanical, more tasteless than such a meal is impossible to imagine;... the seductiveness of a woman asking one to take a meal was altogether beyond her'.[64] On the other hand when they both had a *rendez-vous* with Aymer Maxwell, grandson of a Duke of Northumberland, Canetti notices that 'she was wearing a diaphanous white silk blouse', something he had never seen her do before though she had supposedly been trying to win his love! 'I couldn't hide the truth from myself any more': Canetti concludes, 'she had got herself dolled up for Aymer,... but he wasn't the least bit interested, and just thought she was absurd'. 'But to me she would always come in slovenly academic gear, graceless in her wool or sacking dresses, never really seductive... I had known her for a couple of years at this stage, and never once had she made an effort to make herself attractive to me by wearing any diaphanous silk blouse. I was so astonished that it took me a while to understand'.[65] He self-pityingly concludes: 'It seemed not to have crossed her mind to wonder what it [her seductiveness] might do to me.'

What precisely it did to him is revealed in Iris's journal, whose account differs from his. Soon after this meeting Iris recorded feeling both exasperated and touched by Canetti's warnings that Aymer was a 'werewolf' and 'would do anything he could to drive a wedge between us, even to trying to seduce me. He added, if you do do anything you regret, remember that I am merciful!'[66]

In this trio, Canetti is relieved to surmise, 'Aymer was the lord, I was the "brains", and there wasn't the least space for Iris'. How pathetically Canetti lives up to every expectation of an Iris Murdoch character. His descriptions of her provide a portrait of himself which, in turn, bathes her in reflected glory.

....

64 Ibid p 223.
65 Ibid p 227.
66 Peter Conradi in *the Guardian* reviewing Party in the Blitz, Saturday, July 9th 2005.

'My chief trait, much my strongest quality, which has never been compromised', Canetti persists, 'was the insistence on myself, not at anyone else's expense, but just so: it was always there for me, and saw me through everything'.[67] In other words, as Jeremy Adler suggests, using Richard Ellman's description of Jonathan Swift, 'a mad egoist'. 'Perhaps, if things had happened very differently, I might have been able to love her'.[68] As Iris's cool record predicts, she survived Canetti. Not all his 'creatures' did. Murdoch was, he notes incredulously, the only woman in his life who never sought to capture him. She went on to publish 26 novels, a tally he repeats, 25 more than himself. And she – a woman moreover – won greater literary and social acclaim than he. He terms this – enviously – 'vulgar' success.

But her least forgivable crime I suspect was this: she was the only person who listened more 'greedily' than he. He liked talking better than listening: she spotted and elicited his Mr Toad-like boastfulness. There can be such a thing as 'listener's rape' where the person confiding comes to feel his privacy has been violated, his inner being 'robbed'. Canetti himself gloats over Carol Stewart's and Kathleen Raine's confidences and dependency on him. Murdoch's ultimate crime was to listen, steal and cannibalise her friends' lives with more skill and more inwardness than Canetti.

Further corroboration of this strategy and this technique is provided by Peter Conrad, the Australian born academic who has been teaching Enlish Literature at Oxford University since 1973. In his review of Peter J. Conradi's biography of Iris Murdoch for *The Guardian* in 2001, he describes his thirty year acquaintance with Iris, who would have been twenty-four years older than him [born in 1943], as follows:[69]

---

67   Elias Canetti, *Party in the Blitz*, Harvill Press, London 2005, p 218.
68   Ibid p 221.
69   Peter Conrad, 'Who really knew Iris?' Review of Peter J. Conradi, *Iris Murdoch, A Life* (2001), in The Guardian, 19/9/2001.

My memories of her are still shockingly vivid and intense. That blunt, bold, deliberate handwriting on letters and postcards, like the unjoined-up lettering of a preternaturally intelligent child. The way she once materialised in a corner of my college rooms in Oxford, smiling at me and enjoying the few moments of invisibility she had enjoyed: I yelped when I saw her, as if I had seen a ghost. Her boy-soprano singing voice, which treated me on another occasion to a rendition of 'Waltzing Matilda', and the growly brogue of the same voice in another register when she argued with me. Her helpless laughter, her showers of tears. The way our teeth clashed when she gave me a kiss, and the darting, adder-like sorties (am I being caddish?) of her tongue between my lips... I had my Iris; I had no way of knowing how many others had theirs. She asked questions (and often requested that I tell her three interesting things about my day, which turned me into a storyteller and occasional liar, though it also had the charmed effect of making the dreariest day interesting), but never answered them. Obliquity, evasiveness or downright secrecy kept her multifarious aspects separate. Among the myths she loved was that of Psyche, inducted into heavenly bliss by Cupid, then sworn to silence about forbidden delights. He sealed her lips by placing his finger over them. She illustrated the point with her finger on my face. I understood the embargo, although kisses breached it.

Here is a first-hand account of the seductive yet business-like interview to which many must have been prey in order to fill out the background to her many novels. Conrad made up one of the minor characters in this multitude. But Canetti featured as one of the stars. His major complaint seems to have been that the roles should have been reversed. In 1947, Iris wrote in her journal: 'For me philosophical problems are the problems of my own life'. Conradi's biography makes it clear that Murdoch's life, like her work, was shaped by a moral struggle against forces of destructiveness and sadism. Exhibit A in the laboratory of this exorcism was Elias Canetti. Peter J. Conradi goes further: 'Much that is monstrous in Canetti is symptomatic, or so the novels imply, of what is monstrous in all of us, and in our century'.[70] He sees the war-writings of Canetti and Murdoch and others at the time as bearing out the truism that the world of the twentieth century was in the shadow of Hitler. Many of her best novels have Canetti somewhere behind them, in something of a portrait of Hitler writ small. This would ally her artistry to that of Kafka whom she admired as 'one who sees the forces at work in the world more clearly than we, and so can "prophecy"'.[71]

'Few read Canetti's *Auto-da-Fé* twice. Fewer still read his *Crowds and Power*, with its banalities such as "The Englishman sees himself as captain on board a ship". Murdoch gave it a rare favourable review. Canetti had a cult audience and is now remembered partly because of his liaison with Murdoch. Her worldwide readership remains. Canetti spawned in her not just the mysterious power-broking Mischa Fox, but also demonic puppet-master Julius King in *A Fairly Honourable Defeat*, and rapacious woman-hating tyrant *Charles Arrowby* in her Booker-winning *The Sea, The Sea*. Her answer to Canetti's misogyny is exactly this showroom of monstrously egotistical men. He used to boast that he had helped make her a writer. This was truer than he understood. Where she draws blood in her fiction, a reflection of Canetti can

---

70 Peter J. Conradi, 'Holy Fool and Magus: The Uses of Discipleship in *Under the Net* and *The Flight from the Enchanter*', in *Iris Murdoch, Philosopher, A Collection of Essays* edited by Justin Broackes, Oxford University Press, 2012, Pp. 130-1.

71 In her Sartre, Romantic Rationalist from 1953, quoted by Conradi, op.cit. in *Iris Murdoch, Philosopher, A Collection of Essays* edited by Justin Broackes, Oxford University Press, 2012, p 120.

often be found. "I told her everything," he bitterly laments. Small wonder he came to detest her'.[72]

Another way of decoding the Canettispeak is to examine his heroes. One of the only people in England of whom he approves is Arthur Waley and this because Waley was one of the few who had read and even reviewed Canetti's novel *Die Blendung* (*Auto da Fé*). Waley found that the hero of this book 'had views on women which rather closely matched his own'.[73] '[H]e had no use for women, and had only spoken to Veza because she was standing next to me, and I forced her upon him as my wife'.[74]

Murdoch's project is analysed in a helpful way by both Martha Nussbaum and Maria Antonaccio, but more especially in their combined critique which is summed up pithily in the last chapter of the latter's *A Philosophy to Live By, Engaging Iris Murdoch*, where the author outlines and refines an extended review which Nussbaum wrote of the biography of Iris Murdoch by Peter J. Conradi. The revelations of all the sexual affairs which underpinned both the life and the novels suggested, in the words of Hilary Spurling, that 'Murdoch used her novels to conduct a long and thrilling course of public therapy'. Antonaccio reads Nussbaum as suggesting that 'Murdoch's philosophy represents the outworking of her personal obsessions' and these include her 'personal struggle with her own desire for manipulation and control',[75] her attempt to evade or elude the big fat ego. However, the biography seems to show just how unsuccessful she was in her personal life which draws attention to 'the presence of centralized control' in the novels as well as in life, 'as the characters execute a complicated erotic dance whose choreographer is always just off-stage'. This leads Nussbaum to the 'paradox' that 'attends Murdoch's

---

72   Peter Conradi in the Guardian reviewing *Party in the Blitz*, Saturday, July 9th 2005.
73   Elias Canetti, *Party in the Blitz*, Harvill Press, London 2005, p 143.
74   Ibid p 148.
75   Maria Antonaccio, *A Philosophy to Live By, Engaging Iris Murdoch*, Oxford University Press, 2012, Pp. 245-265.

art': whether the artistic enterprise records and extends the struggle against the ego or whether it is the ego's most subtle victory. If the driving motive of the artistic project is self-perfection and purification... can the gaze of art ever be 'humanly loving' or does it remain 'controlling and manipulative even when it is at its most perceptive'. Antonaccio understands Nussbaum's reading of Murdoch as 'a failed though sincere attempt to domesticate her own narcissistic and destructive sexual impulses'. Antonaccio finds this assessment too psychotherapeutic and reduced. She finds a much more universal and paradigmatic template in the work as a whole. Which means that 'the message to the planet' which Murdoch conveys is not to be found in any or all of her so-called 'philosophical' writings, but in the rich and varied harvest of her artistic oeuvre. 'The work and the life were the same project'.[76] It was only when she was alone in front of her writing desk in the act of creatively transforming her lived experience into the twenty-six stories which she wove so conscientiously in such a comparatively short space of time, that she unleashed that extraordinary capacity to unearth and convey the depths of our human nature. And it is only by studying these novels that we can find the rich understanding of our human reality which it was her gift both to unravel and to weave into a compelling and often hilarious tale. 'Once I've finished a novel IT, not I is telling its story, and one hopes that it will – like some space-probe – go on beaming its message, its light, for some time'.[77] That lonely and dedicated work [seven hours a day when she was 'working'] was something like a creative psychotherapy for humanity. An accurate and subtle hermeneutic of the Murdoch novels, not so much as literature but as 'life', provides the human species with a revealing cardiograph of that most basic energy which motivates us, the way in which we

76 Peter J. Conradi, *Iris Murdoch, A Life*, HarperCollins, London, 2001, p 569.
77 Interview with Susan Hill, Bookshelf, BBC Radio 4, 30 April 1982, quoted in Peter J. Conradi, *Iris Murdoch, A Life*, HarperCollins, London, 2001, P 593.

try to love one another. She was more than our psychotherapist, she was an alchemist. Everything in her life had to be mixed in the flask or crucible of the alchemist, which in the history of that particular art was usually womb-shaped. Alchemy, in this case, is the inner process of creation, the human body providing the flask.

Alchemists believe that base metals in the earth, if penetrated by the sun and processed in the fire of purification can provide gold in the crucible or alembic flask. Love is the agent which eventually brings about this gold. The divine 'gold' of 'love' was imminent in all matter, so, if you poured every chaotic element of life as it presented itself, in whatever combinations might seem possible or relevant at the time of the experiment, and then turned up the heat [*calcinatio* was the technical term for this burning of energy which causes evaporation of volatile constituents and exposes the enduring core] you might find gold. Vulcan the Roman God of fire presided over this furnace, this *athanor*, and is associated with the Greek smith-God Hephaistos, who beat out the shape of your eventual metal. Iris Murdoch distilled through the nib of her pen the underground volcano of emotion created by, with, and through the intense love life which she conscientiously tended as a furnace involving both herself and those who surrounded her. Her own loving was a kind of ontological eros: it sought out in everyone, including herself, the ultimate being of personhood which is the mystery and the attraction of each of us.

Paracelsus, one of the great alchemists, called love the agent of alchemy. He would begin his teaching at the university by placing a stinking pot of hot human excrement on the table saying, 'this is what the work is about, this is all life, this is God'. What goes into such an alembic? Mud, excrement, dragons' teeth, a toad, a bear, the wings of a bat, the leg of a frog, a green dragon, the urine of a mare, everything and anything that makes up the *massa confusa* of reality. Then, after a process of *calcinatio*, which is 'blackening' or burning by fire [Iris often said she wrote two drafts of the novel before getting down to the final configuration], *solutio*, the 'whitening' *albedo*, would occur. This was washing until the elements became dissolved in water. Next was *coagulatio*, the fixing or bringing together in a form, followed by the *sublimatio* or *rubredo*, by which you breathed a higher life, a flesh-and-blood reality, into what you had created making it into a new configuration.

I am using a strange set of images to describe a process quite different from the business of philosophy, a process of creation which involves the unconscious as much as the conscious life. Many other processes from different cultures could be borrowed to introduce and describe the way in which Iris Murdoch transformed the very real stuff of her own extravagant and varied love life into the 'moral' tales which are her legacy, the library of novels which endure. Lao Tsu, describing such a process from the Chinese tradition of the Tao, says: 'The decision to begin must be carried out with a whole heart and the result not sought for. The result will come of itself'.[78]

The two aspects of our human mystery which Murdoch unfurls are 'the strange things which happen when people fall in love'[79] and the even stranger things which happen when people search for God. 'Like Plato and Freud she gave to sexual love and to transformed sexual energy the central place in her thinking. This was the heart of her fiction, as of her philosophy'.[80] Not that the novel form gave her the satisfaction of making a comprehensive synthesis or providing a definitive conclusion which a philosophical treatise might reasonably have expected of her. In 1961 she called

---

78   This quotation and much of what is described here about alchemy is taken from Barbara Somers, *The Fires of Alchemy*, Archive Publishing, Lincolnshire, 2004.
79   A.N.Wilson, *Iris Murdoch as I knew her*, Hutchinson, London, 2003, p 265.
80   Peter J. Conradi, *Iris Murdoch, A Life*, HarperCollins, London, 2001, p 548.

her work 'an investigation that never ends, rather than a means of resolving anything'.[81]

81 Interview with John Barrows, 'Living Writers – 7', John o'London's, 4 May 1961, p 495, quoted by Peter J. Conradi op.cit. p 549.

CHAPTER FOUR

○

Yeats as Yogi

Kathleen Raine, who was born in 1908 and who died at the age of 95 in the year 2003, summed up herself and the century through which she had lived as follows:[1]

> A child of my time, who at Cambridge read Natural Sciences, and rejected my Christian heritage in order to adopt with un-critical zeal the current scientific orthodoxy of that university, I have lived long enough to come full circle. It is all that I learned in my Cambridge days that I have little by little come to reject, by a reversal of premises which has brought me to my own Orient. A slow learner, I have been blessed with a long life which has brought me to a knowledge not taught in our schools.

For W.B. Yeats and for Kathleen Raine, the sages who can teach us a knowledge of another kind are the great poets and visionaries down through the centuries whose wisdom has been harvested in the so-called sacred books from all spiritual traditions. For these two twentieth century protagonists of an alternative world, William Blake (1757-1827) was such a prophet:[2]

> Who beat upon the wall
> Till Truth obeyed his call.

....

1   Kathleen Raine: *W.B. Yeats and the Learning of the Imagination*, Golgonooza Press, 1999 Pp 5-6.
2   W.B. Yeats, 'An Acre of Grass' *Collected Poems*, Macmillan, London, 1955, p 347.

The difficulty is that many people regard William Blake as insane and William Butler Yeats as not much better. Kathleen Raine is dismissed by this widespread constituency as a lesser poet in her dotage, or a semi-religious quack.

Listen to John Carey, Merton Professor at Oxford University and chair of the Man Booker judges for 2004, who is reviewing the first volume of Roy Foster's biography[3] of W.B. Yeats: 'Was he, you find yourself blasphemously wondering, really that intelligent?' and he lists the usual proofs of intellectual backwardness: 'He was substandard at school... He never learnt to spell: even as a grown man, simple monosyllables foxed him... His gullibility was fathomless. Mysticism and magic, to which he was introduced by the half-batty George Russell, occupied much of his waking and sleeping life. He believed he conversed with old Celtic gods and a copious ragbag of other supernaturals'.[4]

Such critics may or may not believe that we have taken a major detour from the path of Truth, but they certainly do not regard William Butler Yeats as a trustworthy guide to a better path, and such critics hold the high ground in influential academic circles.

W.B. Yeats set out to represent an alternative spiritual tradition. His kind of 'prophet' is one whom William Blake would have seen as 'the awakener', one who, like Kathleen Raine, 'speaks *from* the spirit innate in all, *to* the spirit innate in all'.[5]

Yeats wrote to Lady Gregory on the 28 January 1904 describing his first lecture tour in America. He is in Chicago speaking to an almost exclusively Catholic audience in Notre Dame:[6]

3   R.F.Foster, *W.B. Yeats: A Life*, I: The Apprentice Mage 1865-1914, Oxford University Press, 1997; II: The Arch-Poet, 2003.

4   John Carey, 'Poetic License', *The Sunday Times*, 9 March 1997, sec. 8, p.1.

5   Kathleen Raine: *W.B. Yeats and the Learning of the Imagination*, Golgonooza Press, 1999 p 121.

6   *The Letters of W.B. Yeats*, Ed. Alan Wade, 1954, p. 422.

I began of a sudden to think, while I was lecturing, that these Catholic students were so out of the world that my ideas must seem the thunder of a battle fought in some other star ... I think these big priests would be fine teachers, but I cannot think they would be more than that. They belong to an easygoing world that has passed away.

Much of Yeats's life was a battle against the 'easygoing world' which Roman Catholicism seemed to him to represent and which he saw as the paralysing fate of the new Ireland of the twentieth century. He believed that one of his tasks was to provide his country and, indeed, the world of the twentieth century, with the elements of a more vibrant religious life.

I have mummy truths to tell
Whereat the living mock.[7]

These two lines summarize in epigrammatic form the huge ambition and deflating reception of his efforts.

Yeats wrote in his introduction to Lady Gregory's *Gods and Fighting Men* (1904) 'Children at play, at being great and wonderful people' are the true reality of what we are and what we should become. 'Mankind as a whole had a like dream once; everybody and nobody built up the dream bit by bit and the story-tellers are there to make us remember'. But the children of the twentieth century had put away these ambitions 'for one reason or another before they grow into ordinary men and women'. But the poets and the artists and the storytellers are there to keep the dream alive, to keep the path open to that brave new world.

---

7   From the poem 'All Souls' Night, which Yeats wrote at Oxford in the Autumn of 1920, which he included in his book of poems, *The Tower* and used as Epilogue to *A Vision.*

The wisdom which Yeats believed to be our most precious heritage can only be expressed through poetry. The word of God can never be relayed through prose. If this means that the message is sometimes obscure that is not because the poet is being deliberately obscurantist, it is because we are moving in a borderland area for which ordinary language is not designed. Yeats believed also that the whole person in the totality of every constituent part was needed to discover and embody such truth. There is a religion which reneges on its responsibility to discover such Truth and which becomes a search for immunity against the shocks of life. Such a fearful attempt to hide from the demands of human passion and human life is, for Yeats, a denial of the two essential mysteries of Christianity: Creation and Incarnation. Such a religion was the one being proposed, in Yeats's view, for the new Ireland of the twentieth century.

Yeats worked on the text of 'A Vision' for twenty years. It was published in two versions, the first in 1925 the second in 1937, two years before his death. His own 'thinking', if such is the correct term for his work, is neither scientific nor metaphysical, it is mythical. A Vision is a 'gradually accreted credal construct' which finally emerges as a 'massively syncretic mythic system', James Lovic Allen[8] suggested in 1975.

One of the first and most intuitive studies of A Vision by Virginia Moore in 1956, recognizes that Yeats's 'belief' must influence his poetry. However, her analysis never gets beyond the norms of 'good taste' which prescribe for English and American critics that Theosophy is foolishness and all religious mythology eventually Christian.

W.H. Auden was less polite and more dismissive: 'In 1930 we are confronted with the pitiful, the deplorable spectacle of a grown man occupied with the mumbo-jumbo of magic and the nonsense

---

8   James Lovic Allen, 'Belief versus Faith in the Credo of Yeats' *Journal of Modern Literature*, 4, 1975, pp 692-716.

of India'.[9] And elsewhere: 'All these absurd books', and with his irritatingly superior snigger: 'but mediums, spells, the Mysterious Orient – how embarrassing'.[10] Hugh Kenner granted it, in 1956, the architectural status of a 'gothic fortress' which a brief generation of critics had assaulted and 'scrutinizing its interior by periscope reported that it was full of bats'.[11] Northrop Frye called it 'an infernal nuisance' that we 'can't pretend doesn't exist'.

Critics in the 1960s became more cautious and respectful. Helen Vendler[12] tried to rehabilitate it as a source of poetic imagery, an experience necessary to produce the power of the later poetry and the plays of the mature artist. Harold Bloom, acknowledging the sympathetic brilliance of her salvage operation, wishes he could agree, but cannot: 'Jung is a bad romantic poet, Yeats a great one who suffered, in A Vision, a failure in vision'.[13] Ellmann prolongs the architectural metaphor in 1967: 'A Vision is a cathedral whose "symbolic portentousness" seems to liquidate humanity and into which its author is suctioned, "cocooned" or ingested'.[14] Steven Helming in 1977 suggests that the whole thing is a hoax which confounds all Yeats's enemies and critics and shows him to be a comic genius almost as cunning and perverse as Joyce.[15] Matthew De Forrest in 1991 presents the intriguing possibility that the book is in code form and that, like the esoteric subjects with which it deals, unfolds itself in a secret language for those who can read the signs. The surface narrative is a decoy to deflect cynics and scoffers.[16] Perhaps the most useful work

9   W.H.Auden, 'Prosecution and defence' quoted in Elizabeth Butler Cullingford, *Gender and History in Yeats's love poetry*, Cambridge, 1993, p.249.
10   W.H.Auden, *The Permanence of Yeats*, 1961.
11   Hugh Kenner, 'Unpurged Images', *The Hudson Review*, 8, 1956.
12   Helen Vendler, *Yeats's Vision and the Later Plays*, 1963.
13   Harold Bloom, *Yeats*, 1970.
14   Richard Ellmam, *Eminent Domain: Yeats among Wilde, Joyce, Pound, Eliot and Auden*, 1967, p 80.
15   Steven Helmling, 'Yeats's Esoteric Comedy', *The Hudson Review*, 30, 1977, Pp 230-246.
16   Matthew De Forrest, as yet unpublished MA Thesis, University College Dublin, 1991.

was done by A. Norman Jeffares whose biography of W.B. Yeats[17] and 1990 edition of *A Vision* and related writings,[18] put the texts and the facts at the disposal of anyone interested, in a practical, dispassionate way. At the beginning of the twenty-first century a wealth of biographical and critical work help us to take a more measured and sympathetic stance.

The variety of bemused interpretation and irritated skepticism which have surrounded *A Vision* ever since its creation, are caused, or at least exacerbated, by the coy and deliberate fiction with which Yeats surrounded the origins of this work. The 1925 edition was presented as the essential teaching of an Arabian tribe, the Judwali, who had once possessed a learned book called *The Way of the Soul between the Sun and the Moon* attributed to a certain Kusta ben Luka, a Christian Philosopher at the Court of Harun Al-Raschid. This sacred book had been lost and its essential doctrine was explained to younger members of the tribe through the medium of diagrams drawn by old religious men upon the sand. These diagrams were identical with a book called *Speculum Angelorum et Hominorum* which had been written by a certain Giraldus and printed in Cracow in 1594. Two old friends of Yeats, with whom he had quarrelled, Michael Robartes and Owen Aherne meet in the National Gallery in 1917. Robartes is in possession of this wisdom collected in 'sheets of paper which were often soiled and torn... rolled up in a bit of old camel skin and tied in bundles with bits of cord and bits of shoe-lace. This bundle... described the mathematical law of history, that bundle the adventure of the soul after death and that other the interaction between the living and the dead'.

17   A. Norman Jeffares, *W.B. Yeats, A New Biography*, 1988, Arena Paperback Edition, 1990.
18   A. Norman Jeffares, *W.B. Yeats, 'A Vision' and Related Writings, 1989*, Arena Paperback Edition, 1990.

Michael Robartes is in possession of the wisdom which he wants Owen Aherne to publish. The trouble is that 'no man has ever had less gift of expression' than Robartes, and Aherne is incapable of receiving the wisdom without imposing upon it his own Christian interpretation. The two quarrel violently and Robartes decides that they should give the documents to Yeats and ask him to write them down. Robartes had originally intended to do this but baulked at the prospect, saying to Aherne: 'I have great gifts in my hands and I stand between two enemies; Yeats that I quarrelled with and have not forgiven; you that quarrelled with me and have not forgiven me'.

In the second edition of 1937, Yeats admits that this introduction was made up by him because the real truth of the origin of *A Vision* involved his wife and she had not been prepared to have her name associated with the text at that time. Now, he is able to tell the real story: Four days after his marriage when he was in a state of gloom, mostly because he was thinking of Maud Gonne and her daughter Iseult, his wife began to act as a medium, through a process of automatic writing, and this was the beginning of those revelations which he later edited into their final form in *A Vision*. He describes the strange occurence of these revelations in the Introduction to the second edition, under the heading 'A Packet for Ezra Pound': 'What came in disjointed sentences, in almost illegible writing, was so exciting, sometimes so profound, that I persuaded her to give an hour or two day after day to the unknown writer, and after some half-dozen such hours offered to spend what remained of life explaining and piecing together those scattered sentences. "No," was the answer, "we have come to give you metaphors for poetry."'

Early readers of these texts can be forgiven for suspecting that the whole thing was humbug, and for accusing Mrs Yeats of inventing her mediumship as a way of shaking her husband out of a depression four days after their marriage.

It would have been difficult for the average Irish person in the forties and fifties of the last century to understand the relationship between Yeats and his wife Georgie Hyde-Lees. He married her at the age of 52 when she was 26, in the same year during which he had already proposed to Maud Gonne for the umpteenth time and to her daughter, Iseult for at least the second time. Maud Gonne and he had been 'mystically' married according to themselves, and Yeats remained obsessed by her throughout his life. Yeats also had several love affairs before and after he was married. Such facts are hard for those of us who live in 'an easygoing world that has passed away' to understand; they certainly sound like 'thunder of a battle fought in some other star'.

According to Yeats's own account:[19]

> I was saying to myself, 'I have betrayed three people', then I thought, 'I have lived all through this before'. Then George spoke of the sensation of having lived through something before (she knew nothing of my thought). Then she said she felt that something was to be written through her. She got a piece of paper, and talking to me all the while so that her thoughts would not affect what she wrote, wrote these words (which she did not understand), 'with the bird' (Iseult) 'all is well at heart. Your action was right for both but in London you mistook its meaning'.

To suggest that either or both these extraordinary people were guilty of fraud in these circumstances is to misunderstand the reality which is being touched upon here. Mrs Yeats was a much more creative and impressive partner to W.B. in all their many pursuits together than early uninformed gossip and speculation allowed. Her

---

19 Letter to Lady Gregory, 29 October 1917, Alan Wade, op.cit.

portrait emerges much more positively in the biography of Yeats by
A. Norman Jeffares who describes her as

> very well educated, being a good linguist by aptitude and very
> well read ... They had a lot in common. She was studying as-
> trology... Like many of his friends, she shared his interest in
> tarot cards. She was reading philosophy. She was attending sé-
> ances with him and she was admitted – probably in 1914, with
> Yeats as sponsor – to the *Stella Matutina* section of the Golden
> Dawn'.[20]

They were together in the making of *A Vision* and research by
George Mills Harper presents us with over 4,000 pages which were
transmitted through Georgie Yeats, sometimes while she was asleep
but mostly while she was awake. More subtle instruments and methods are needed to understand this phenomenon. Both Margaret Mills
Harper and Elizabeth Butler Cullingford hold that many of the seminal ideas of *A Vision* originated in the mind of George Yeats and that
its communal genesis destroys the possibility of individual authorship or control over the text.[21] Ann Saddlemeyer's biography of Mrs
W.B. Yeats establishes all this authoritatively.[22]

Whatever we say about *A Vision* we have to recognize that both
Yeats and his wife believed that the text came to them from 'unknown
instructors' in a dimension other than our workaday consciousness.
It represented the event for which Yeats had been waiting and pre-
paring himself during all the weary and frustrating hours of discipleship to various orders and societies. It was a moment of revelation

20 A. Norman Jeffares, *W.B. Yeats, A New Biography*, Arena Paperback Edition, 1990,
    p 146 & p 175.
21 Elizabeth Butler Cullingford, *Gender and history in Yeats's love poetry*, Cambridge,
    1993, p 106.
22 Anne Saddlemeyer, *Becoming George, The Life of Mrs W.B. Yeats*, Oxford University
    Press, 2002.

during which Yeats 'received' a wisdom which he felt bound to record without interpretation or elaboration. His reception of it was dependent upon his wife and at the time of their commitment to this audition they experienced a blending of their souls which put them in touch with a much larger psychic reality, stretching both in time and in space beyond the limited circumference of the historical life of each or of both of them. This, then, is the source of *A Vision*. That one of its results was to inspire Yeats to more effective poetic endeavour seems also to be indisputable. The structure of *The Tower*, the book of poetry he published in 1928, is based upon the revelations which also informed the work he called *A Vision*. The book of poetry was named both for the poem of that title, and Thoor Ballylee, the ancient tower house which still stands and which Yeats and his wife were converting into a symbolic home for themselves. Yeats wanted this book of poetry, named after Thoor Ballylee, to be an icon in itself, and as itself. The real tower in which he lived, and the book of poems called after it, were the most important legacy he would leave behind him. He had asked Sturge Moore to create the design for the cover: 'The Tower should not be too unlike the real object or rather... it should suggest the real object. I like to think of that building as a permanent symbol of my work plainly visible to the passer-by'.[23] Both the building and the book are congruent to the structure of *A Vision*, published three years earlier in 1925. The poem 'All Souls' Night' serves as epilogue to both books.

The question which haunts in the presence of such texts is: are we here in possession of something which has succeeded in pushing back a little further the frontiers of human ignorance? Has Yeats's genius, coupled with the genius of his wife, allowed all of us to make a break-through to areas which had been unavailable to the realm of human discourse? Is this writing something in the order of a prophe-

---

23   *W.B.Yeats and T. Sturge Moore: Their Correspondence 1901-37*, ed. Ursula Bridge, Oxford University Press, 1953, p 114.

cy heralding a new age of religious consciousness? This is what Yeats fervently believed and this is what it is our duty to explore. In the touchingly arrogant words of our potential master, speaking of 'Ireland and the Arts', and quoting his friend Mr Ellis: 'It is not the business of a poet to make himself understood, but it is the business of people to understand him. That they are at last compelled to do so is the proof of his authority.'[24]

Are we to take *A Vision* seriously on its own terms, on Yeats's terms? If so, then it is a revolutionary document; if not, it may be of interest to literary criticism but it is not essential to life. In examining the total phenomenon we must recognize both its dual authorship and the particular poetic genius of the one who gave it definitive and enduring expression. Yeats was essentially a poet and all his great work is given to us in the language of poetry. The text of *A Vision* is, therefore, irretrievably connected to Mrs W.B. Yeats as source, and to the later poems and plays of W.B. Yeats as collateral.

Terence Brown's captures certain nuances and subtleties in this regard. 'To the institution of an occult marriage', he suggests, 'Yeats as poet owed a great debt, as do we his readers, who discover in his later writings a body of work which confronts in its heroic and radically disturbing fashion, the crisis faced by the religious imagination in the modern world'.[25]

When we ask why did Yeats not come out into the open and say to his readers: 'I am a prophet. I have just received a divine revelation which I am now communicating to you in a work called *A Vision*, which has taken much of my life to elaborate in its now definitive form, and which, of all my works, is the one containing the most important wisdom it has been given to me to impart',[26] we must look

24   W.B. Yeats, *Essays and Introductions*, 1961, p 207.
25   Terence Brown, *The Life of W.B. Yeats*, Gill & Macmillan, Dublin, 1999, p 266.
26   As indeed he wrote in a private letter to T.Werner Laurie, 20th April, 1924, quoted by Anne Saddlemeyer, op.cit. p 341: 'Such wisdom of life, results of much toil and concentration, as has been granted me, that part of me that is a creative mystic, that made out of the shadow of Swedenborg is in this book'.

for answers in at least three sensitive areas: Yeats's awareness of the hostility of others, and his own timidity and lack of self-confidence. These were little appreciated facts at the time, but have been perceptively presented by one of his early biographers, Richard Ellman. Denis Donoghue sums it up:[27]

> In Ireland, it is fair to say, Yeats is resented; not for his snobbery, his outlandish claim to the possession of Norman blood, or even for his evasion of history by appeal to two classes of people who existed only as shades – Gaelic Irish and Anglo-Irish – but because he claimed to speak in the name of 'the indomitable Irishry'. De Valera claimed to speak for Ireland, and the claim was tenable: he has had, in that capacity, no successor. In the present confusions, readers of Yeats resent his appeal to Irishness, and his assertion that he knows the quality of Irishness when he meets it. That resentment is so inclusive that little or nothing survives in its presence.

According to Elizabeth Butler Cullingford, 'Yeats knew that his name had become a byword for paganism, anti-Catholicism, opposition to Gaelic culture, and snobbery' among his Catholic counterparts, and especially in the Catholic culture being supported and diffused by such publicity organs as *The Catholic Bulletin*.[28]

Roy Foster's biography[29] shows the persistence and depth of antagonism between Catholic Ireland, as incarnated in the newly established Free State and expressed in *The Catholic Bulletin*, and the 'New Ascendancy' which they saw as 'epitomized by people like

27   *We Irish, Essays on Irish Literature and Society*, University of California Press, 1986, Pp 66.
28   Elizabeth Butler Cullingford, *Gender and history in Yeats's love poetry*, Cambridge, 1993, P 144.
29   R.F.Foster, *W.B. Yeats: A Life*, I: The Apprentice Mage 1865-1914, Oxford University Press, 1997; II: The Arch-Poet, 2003.

WBY, Gogarty, Plunkett, and Russell, and entrenched in institutions such as the Royal Irish Academy, Trinity College, and the Senate'. The Bulletin described the Nobel Prize which Yeats won in 1923 as 'the substantial sum provided by a deceased anti-Christian manufacturer of dynamite'. 'It is common knowledge', this report continues, 'that the line of recipients of the Nobel prize shows that a reputation for Paganism in thought and word is a very considerable advantage in the sordid annual race for money, engineered, as it always is, by clubs, coteries, salons and cliques'.[30]

Secondly, Yeats was obsessed by mysticism, in awe of those whom he knew to be geniuses in this sphere, and aware that he was not one of these, but rather a poet. Those who idolize the man and worship his poetry find it difficult to understand this hierarchy of values. However, the circle of Yeats's most intimate friends shared it. In this esoteric work, which Yeats fostered for most of his life with dedication and energy, there were others who were more gifted and capable than he was. Yeats was interested in creating a Celtic Order of Mysteries which would 'select its symbols from all the things that had moved men "through many, mainly Christian, centuries"'.[31] However, Yeats seemed to have been aware at all times of his dependence upon others for his own mystical life. He was something of an orphan in the spiritual realm and did not possess the self-contained visionary faculty which, he believed, others like AE, Blake and MacGregor Mathers embodied. Yeats's wife said when AE died that he was 'the nearest to a saint you and I will ever meet'. She was addressing her husband, and went on to say, 'You are a better poet, but no saint'.

Thirdly, Yeats was brought up by his father, whom he 'admired ... above all men', as an enlightened agnostic. Darwin and Huxley had put paid to Christianity and all the superstitious mythology of pre-scientific humanity. The discoveries which ushered in the twen-

---

30   Foster, II (2003) p 256.
31   A. Norman Jeffares, *W.B. Yeats, A New Biography*, Arena Paperback Edition, 1990, p 77.

tieth century in both science and art allowed John Butler Yeats to be optimistically humanist. He wanted his children to avail of the freedom and knowledge to which they now had a right, and was anxious to defend them from the destructive and guilt-ridden complexes which established churches had foisted upon their contemporaries. John B. Yeats's biographer suggests that had he lived to read *A Vision*, 'the shock would surely have killed him'.[32]

His son believed that true Christianity should be grafted to the indigenous religion of a country, that each country became a 'Holy Land' only when its imagination had been captured and its Old Testament led towards the expansive and comprehensive fulfilment of the new. Europe had no older or greater religious tradition than that embodied in the rites, the sites, the pilgrimages of prechristian, Celtic Ireland.

Byzantium, which symbolized for Yeats that perfect fusion of Christianity with the human imagination, in its early period, was contemporaneous with St Patrick (396-469). The 'unity of being' within a 'unity of culture' which Yeats regarded as the goal of religious reconciliation, was evident in the Book of Kells and other art works of this period of Celtic culture.[33] One of the major differences between this earlier Christianity and later manifestations of it, especially in the version being institutionalized in Ireland after independence, but also in various protestant variations, was its capacity to integrate the sexual as a sacred mystery central to all life of whatever kind. The character of Crazy Jane in Yeats's imagination represents the Old Testament of the Celtic race crying out against the bishop, representing institutionalized religion, especially its contemporary Irish Catholic variety. Sexual prudery and puritanism were major enemies in Yeats's crusade for a more integrated and wholesome Christianity.

....

32 William Murphy quoted in Brenda Maddox, *George's Ghosts, A New Life of W.B. Yeats*, Picador, London, 1999, p 204
33 Cf Kathleen Raine, *Yeats the Initiate*, London, 1986.

There is sufficient evidence to suggest that the source of Yeats's mystical writings is the blending of the collective unconscious with the corporate personality achieved by his wife and himself through satisfactory sexual communion, involving frequent intercourse which had to include female orgasm. 'Collaboration between the sexes was the enabling precondition of Yeats's achievement, and the topic of sexual love dominated his conversation with the spirits'.[34]

The sexual was 'the sixth sense' which could tune into the unconscious, creating the balance between creativity and sexuality which brought about 'unity of being'. Anne Saddlemeyer has provided the most convincing account of this common source of 'the script' which was communicated to W.B. Yeats and his wife George during so many hours of their married life.[35] Such contact with the sacred is germane to a long tradition of mystical experience which, even in the Judaeo-Christian versions, from the book of Genesis, through the Song of Songs, to the writings of so many poets of mystical 'marriage', employs the image of male/female union to describe relationship with the divine.

Elizabeth Butler Cullingford sees the 'Supernatural Songs' which were written after Yeats had had an operation to restore his sexual potency, as 'the verses of a ribald iconoclast who is out to disturb musty piety, but is nevertheless serious about reconciling divine love with the natural emotion of human passion'.[36] She also suggests that Yeats found in Indian Tantric philosophy 'the acceptance of sex as a road to divinity' and an affirmation of his own insistence upon 'an alliance between body and soul' which 'our theology rejects'.[37]

....

34   Elizabeth Butler Cullingford, *Gender and history in Yeats's love poetry*, Cambridge, 1993, P 111 f.
35   Anne Saddlemeyer, *Becoming George, The Life of Mrs W.B. Yeats*, Oxford University Press, 2002, Pp 119-123.
36   Elizabeth Butler Cullingford, op.cit. p 248.
37   Ibid p 253.

Yeats's work in *A Vision* is the desert geometry, the abstract sketch, the 'frozen music', which his later work fleshes out. The poem 'The Gift of Harun Al-Rashid' explains the relationship between the poet's marriage and his initiation into the mysteries which constitute *A Vision*. It tells the story of Yeats's marriage at the age of 52 with a young woman and how the ensuing ecstasy revealed through her, was nothing less than the infrastructure of the universe. The extraordinary world into which both he and his partner were introduced, through the everyday event of their sexual communion, is also conveyed by the unreal and antique nature of the story. As Yeats had said of Maud Gonne that his earlier poetry 'shadowed in a glass/ What thing her body was' so *A Vision* was a cubist representation of the body of his wife. 'The Gift of Harun Al-Rashid' is possibly the nearest we shall get to unscrambling that cubist encodement. 'Perhaps', as he said in 1934, 'now that the abstract intellect has split the mind into categories, the body into cubes, we may be about to turn back towards the unconscious, the whole, the miraculous'.[38]

Anne Saddlemeyer's painstaking biography of George Yeats has shown too that she was, perhaps, the more important partner in the eventual achievement of the scripts. Yeats regarded himself as both the dispositive and the final cause of these revelations. He believed that it depended on him to make whatever use might be made of their common 'script'. But the script as it finally emerged is probably more beholden to George's contributions than it is to W.B.'s, although neither he nor she, nor for that matter any of the critics, would have believed this; nor would they have any interest in it – the only important thing about it was the affect it had on one of the great poets of the twentieth century.

The marriage of Yeats and George Hyde-Lees was more a sacred tryst than a romantic alliance. She was, in fact, the perfect partner to

38   W.B. Yeats, *Explorations*, Selected by Mrs W.B. Yeats, Macmillan, London, 1962 p 404.

the apprentice mage and his union with her was probably the most important energy in his life both as person and as poet. His connection with Maud Gonne and her daughter Iseult was more absorbing and stimulating in terms of literary gossip, romantic obsession and early poetry, but the deep sexual intimacy of his relationship with George was of a different order and became the source of whatever happiness he achieved, mystical insight he attained, and great poetry and drama of his later years.

A *Vision* is the map of another country. It is a country to which access was given to Yeats through sexual communion with his wife. It is a country which is wider and deeper than individual consciousness. In their case it became apparent that she began to speak the words from a more extensive consciousness, shared by at least the two of them, but more importantly extending beyond even this expansion of normal understanding, to one shared by the dead. It holds and provides an imagery, a geometry, a symbolism which can be shared by those who have gone before us. It allows the possibility of communion, commensalism with the dead. It goes further and suggests that there is a whole area of consciousness, not just between birth and death, but between death and birth, which can be logged into by an art which lures us to the borders of trance. In itself A *Vision* does not 'do' this. Art is the doer of such deeds.

Yeats's ghosts told him that they were bringing him images for poetry. This has often been interpreted as a diminishment in religious terms of his original project in the work of A *Vision*. Such interpretion reads the statement as dismissal of the whole occult experience in his life and his marriage as simply convoluted and fantastic pantomimes and gymnastics to provide him with paraphernalia for his poems, animals for his circus. However, the statement can be understood differently.

Providing images for poetry can be more than fodder for a harvester. Images are not simply manageable units to be included within a predictable tapestry. Images are like diamonds which need the expertise of poetry to display in their multifacetted polyvalence. And here we have to take seriously the parallel work of Ezra Pound, who influenced not only Yeats but also T.S. Eliot and many other pioneers of twentieth century poetic practice, especially in his almost neurotic attempt to guide this particular idiom through the movements of 'imagisme' first of all, and then 'vorticism', to prevent it from being contaminated by lesser, more popular and thereby more compromising versions of itself.

Pound had defined the Image as 'that which presents an intellectual and emotional complex in an instant of time' and later expanded this attempt to corrall and to brand the original species of wildness which he knew had been eliminated almost to the point of extinction by the twentieth century manufacturers of thought, and which he believed passionately it was the task of the poet to revive and to rehabilitate. 'The Image is more than an idea. It is a vortex or cluster of fused ideas and is endowed with energy. If it does not fulfil these specifications, it is not what I mean by an Image'.[39]

So, when we say that the later poems of Yeats were vehicles for the Images which he received from the 20 year process of religious endeavour, recorded more prosaically in A Vision, we are saying more than that the contents of these poems are full of strange and bizarre pictures which make them more piquant and esoteric. Yeats is attempting to formulate an inspiration received from elsewhere in a shape and structure of language which demand an originality, an ingenuity as idiosyncratic and pliable as that employed by Byzantine artisans, required and permitted for the first time to hammer out the mystery of a God become Man.

We have been educated out of myth and magic. We are able to symbolise as children but this faculty is erased by our learning the

---

39   Quoted in *Imagist Poetry*, ed. Peter Jones, Penguin Books, 1972, p 40.

three Rs, our so-called system of education. Civilised societies of the twentieth century democratised the languages of reading and writing. These became fundamental currency in the West. They also became the criteria for 'intelligence' as we see from the above assessment of W.B. Yeats by professors at Oxford in recent years. Only those who have fallen between the bars of the grid know the extent to which they are marginalized and deprived by illiteracy. We imagine that reading and writing are natural to us, whereas, in fact, they must be two of the most unnatural activities ever undertaken by creatures on this planet.

People of Western Europe in the twentieth century were not only able to read and write more or less instinctively, they translated everything that presented itself to them into this narrow network. We read music, art, cinema, life and love. Everything we did was a story, an alphabet, a grammar, a plot, a chapter, a closed book, a best seller. We read and we wrote our lives. My diary was my day translated into linear modules of coherent literacy. From four years of age all our children are condemned to a bookish, commercial education. Recent meetings of the United Nations seem determined to inflict this myopia on all children of the world in the name of equality of opportunity and universal education.

Walter Ong[40] has examined this restricted vision in much detail. He shows how a languge such as High Latin which was never a 'mother tongue' [taught by one's mother] to later generations of Europeans, became their only access to so-called Higher Education. Obviously Latin was once a spoken language but it became a 'school language', completely controlled by writing, once it ceased to be a vernacular tongue for those who used it. It became the *lingua franca* of the universities based in academia and suffusing an exclusively male environment.

....
40   Walter J. Ong, *Orality and Literacy, The Technologizing of the Word*, Routledge, London & New York, 1982, This Edition, 2000 Hereafter in this text referred to as [Ong + page number].

For well over a thousand years [Latin] was sex-linked, a language written and spoken only by males, learned outside the home in a tribal setting which was in effect a male puberty rite setting, complete with physical punishment and other kinds of deliberately imposed hardships. It had no direct connection with anyone's unconscious of the sort that mother tongues, learned in infancy, always have... Devoid of baby-talk, insulated from the earliest life of childhood where language has its deepest psychic roots, a first language to none of its users, pronounced across Europe in often mutually unintelligible ways but always written the same way, Learned Latin was a striking exemplification of the power of writing for isolating discourse and of the unparalleled productivity of such isolation... making possible the exquisitely abstract world ofmedieval scholasticism and of the new mathematical modern science which followed on the scholastic experience. Without Learned Latin, it appears that modern science would have got under way with greater difficulty, if it had got under way at all. Modern science grew in Latin soil, for philosophers and scientists through the time of Sir Isaac Newton commonly both wrote and did their abstract thinking in Latin [Pp 113-114].

Only those, like W.B. Yeats for instance, escaped the net and retained their imaginative faculties by default. Only those marginalised from our education system stumbled upon the alternative and, in many cases, became what we term great artists or geniuses of one kind or another. Yeats's intelligence was essentially mythic. Such intelligence weaves its way through symbols and has a very different perspective on the universe from that of the scientist, for instance. Our generation has been innoculated against such balderdash.

A seminal work in providing such awareness of our symbolic blindness is *The Crane Bag and other Essays* by Robert Graves.[41] The title essay is the review by Graves of a book by Dr Anne Ross called *Pagan Celtic Britain*. Graves believes that this highly qualified academic celtologist is barred from understanding the very material she is writing about because of her university education and scientific mentality. 'As a girl of seventeen Dr Ross had done what anthropologists call "field-work" by learning Gaelic for six months in a West Highland peasant's hut. Then after graduating at Edinburgh, she took an educational job in the same Goidelic region, but later returned to Edinburgh for a degree in Celtic studies and a Ph.D. in Celtic archaeology'. Thus, according to Graves 'she forgot... how to think in Gaelic Crofter style, which means poetically'. He makes his point by quoting her treatment of an important Celtic Myth about 'The Crane Bag' of the sea-god Manannan Mac Lir. This bag had been made for the Sea-God from the skin of a woman magically transformed into a crane. 'This crane-bag held every precious thing that Manannan possessed. The shirt of Manannan himself and his knife, and the shoulder-strap of Goibne, the fierce smith, together with his smith's hook; also the king of Scotland's shears; and the King of Lochlainn's helmet; and the bones of Asil's swine. A strip of the great whale's back was also in that shapely crane-bag. When the sea was full, all the treasures were visible in it; when the fierce sea ebbed, the crane-bag was empty'.

Dr Ross is like the rest of us, trained out of our poetic sensibility. She has lost the art of reading the signs of the times. According to Graves she 'can make nothing of such fairy-tale material'. He has to interpret for her: 'What the fabulous Crane Bag contained was alphabetical secrets known only to oracular priests and poets. The inspiration came, it is said, from observing a flock of cranes, "which make letters as they fly". And Hermes, messenger to the Gods, afterwards

41   Robert Graves, *The Crane Bag and Other Essays*, Cassell: London, 1969, Pp 1-8.

reduced these to written characters. Cranes were in fact totem birds of the poetically educated priests... That the Crane Bag filled when the sea was in flood, but emptied when it ebbed, means that these Ogham signs made complete sense for the poetic sons of Manannan, but none for uninitiated outsiders. The Crane Bag was not, in fact, a tangible object, but existed only as a metaphor'.

Dr Ross as an academic archaeologist has the job of digging up 'things' from the past, dating and comparing these. But as a trained scientist 'she can accept no poetic or religious magic'. Anything that falls outside the scope of her 'academic conditioning' is 'branded as mythical – mythical being, like Pagan, a word that denies truth to any ancient non-Christian emblem, metaphor or poetic anecdote'. We too have been overly trained in scientific prejudices. We no longer see the world as symbol. We are incapable of reading the signs of the times, of unearthing the Spirit at work in our world. Our world is like the island of Shakespeare's *Tempest*: a confusion of bewildering lights and sounds to Caliban, but 'clear signals from a different order of experience' to Prospero's eyes and ears. We have to decide whether 'to turn tail on it all like howling Caliban or to develop new powers of attention and perception capable of orchestrating this mad music'.[42]

Symbolic intimation in poetic form is Yeats's strategy of expression. 'We would seek out those wavering, meditative, organic rhythms, which are the embodiment of the imagination' he proposes in the 'Symbolism of Poetry'. This idiosyncratic and comprehensive idiom has been masterfully examined by Denis Donoghue:[43] 'His instrument is rhythm, presumably because human feeling, which seeks release in words and is outraged by the poor release it finds, sways to rhythm as to music'.

....
42   Alan McGlashan, *Savage and Beautiful Country*, Hillstone, New York, 1966.
43   *We Irish, Essays on Irish Literature and Society*, University of California Press, 1986, Pp 35 –51

Yeats learnt much from Arthur Symons who dedicated his book *The Symbolist Movement in Literature* (1899) to him. 'To name is to destroy, to suggest is to create', was Mallarmé's principle, according to Symons, and the most subtle instrument of suggestion was rhythm, 'which is the executive soul'. Sartre has argued in his Preface to Mallarmé's *Poésies* that Mallarmé's devotion to the imaginary arises from his resentment against reality, and the poems written in that mood are symbolic acts of revenge: the poet's words are designed to undo the work of the first Creation, the poem being a second and higher version.

> 'An image becomes a symbol', Donoghue explains, 'on being touched by value or significance not attributable to its own set. For example: think of an event in narrative as a moment or a position along a line, straight or crooked, and then think of it as being crossed by another line of value from another source. Each line is a set, a paradigm. But the event which occurs at the point of intersection between two sets is an image in both; its duplicity constitutes its symbolic force. Interpreted in one set, it declares itself unrestrained by that interpretation; it is part of the other set as well. When we find an image becoming a symbol, we feel in it this double potency; its allegiance expands, as if answerable to both idioms, ready to participate in both sets of relations. This marks its freedom and its suggestiveness; we have a sense in attending to it that there is no point at which we can say for sure that its force has come to an end'.[44]

44 Ibid.

However, Donoghue suggests, 'Yeats started out as a Symbolist and ended as something else'. In 'The Symbolism of Poetry' Yeats says that

> all sounds, all colours, all forms, either because of their pre-ordained energies or because of long association, evoke inde-finable and yet precise emotions, or, as I prefer to think, call down among us certain disembodied powers, whose footsteps over our hearts we call emotions.

And in 'The Philosophy of Shelley's Poetry' he speaks of the Great Memory as 'a dwelling-house of symbols, of images that are living souls'. Therefore 'the aura we feel in the symbol' marks for Yeats the presence of the supernatural in the natural. The poet is therefore a mage, adept in secret but traditional knowledge. The poet must become an alchemist of the word. Symbolism is the poet's form of magic, except that what the mage does consciously the poet does half consciously and half by instinct. The ancient secret is common to both disciplines. Magic was congenial to Yeats's mind for many reasons, but especially because it exerted the heuristic [serving to discover; *heur* = 'find' in Greek] power of language, the common grammar of mage and poet.

This goes some way to account for the incantatory note in Yeats's hieratic style, where his lines are more readily acceptable if we take them as rituals, prescriptions, or interdictions than as secular utter-ances delivered from a high horse. Morton Irving Seiden[45] suggests that Yeats saw great art in general and his own poems in particular as embodiments of the supernatural. His symbols have theurgical pow-er; his poems and plays are sacred rites. 'In a number of his essays, but notably in "Speaking to the Psaltery", first published in 1902, he

45   Morton Irving Seiden, *The Poet as a Mythmaker 1865-1939*, Michigan State University Press, 1962, Pp 286-7.

urges that his poems be chanted or intonated as though they were (it seems) Orphic prayers'. By means of these supernatural poems 'he tried to recreate in the modern world the mythologies of ancient India, Eleusian Greece, and pre-Christian Ireland'.

The ring-master in this circus of imagery has a task as complicated as shunting carriage loads of sparkling and exploding jewelry along converging railway lines from a signal box at a junction in an antique railway station. The signal box or cabin from which all such direction occurred was called, appropriately, 'The Tower'. Originally all such signalling was done by mechanical means: cables or rods, connected at one end to the signals and at the other to the signal box, run alongside the railway. The guts of such a system is a signalling frame, complex cabling arrangements with linkage to levers and controls. A railroad switch is an installation at a point where one rail track divides into two further tracks. It can be set in either of two positions, determining whether a train coming from A will be led to B or to C. If we adapt this image to the 'system' which Yeats was trying to install, we find him in a Tower overlooking a junction where many more than three 'trains of thought' are merging. 'Central to the development of this elliptical and mysterious series', says Foster about the poem 'A last Confession', for instance, 'is the subtle patterning whereby the interpenetrating gyres and cones of occult astrology are equated to the physical act of love: a fusion of the spiritual and the erotic which for WBY connects not only to Swedenborgian cosmology but also to his early (and future) interest in Indian philosophy'.[46]

The Image is the vehicle, almost the stunt artist, which allows such ambidexterity to be conveyed without losing its integrity or betraying its illusivity. Can it be translated into logical thought? Helen Vendler certainly thinks so. Her book, *Poets Thinking*,[47] defends poet-

---

46   R.F.Foster, *W.B. Yeats: A Life*, Oxford University Press, Volume II: The Arch-Poet, 2003, p 319.
47   Helen Vendler, *Poets Thinking*, Harvard University Press, 2004.

ry, because it is 'a feat of ordered language' as, therefore, 'something one can only call thought'.[48] Her 'criticism' of poetry has tried to elucidate the thinking of a poem as 'an exemplification of its own inner momentum' and in her chapter on 'W.B. Yeats Thinking' she claims to have cracked the code of his system of thought which she calls 'Thinking in Images' and which she uses as the subtitle of the same chapter. In justice, she claims 'we must call what [poets] do, in the process of conceiving and completing the finished poem, an intricate form of thinking, even if it means expanding our idea of what thinking is'. This 'thinking' cannot be revealed by 'a thematic paraphrase' for instance, but it can be excavated by the conscientious critic. Such a critic must be able to translate the subtle calculus of concatenated imagery into however distended an epistemology. What she describes as 'the complex architectonic assembling of images by Yeats' can be shown as his 'style of thinking' because even though it may become 'instinctual' in 'the heat of composition' it still 'issues from an extensive repertoire of image-memory and intellectual invention, coupled with an uncanny clairvoyance with respect to emotional experience'.[49] So, 'if we are to understand a poem, we must reconstruct the anterior thinking [always in process, always active] that generated its surface, its "visible core"'.[50] Such 'thinking', described as 'the evolving discoveries of the poem', Vendler admits 'can be grasped only by our participating in the process they unfold'. However, in my view, she has already prejudiced such participation by limiting it to four comprehensive fields which she names as 'psychological, linguistic, historical, philosophical'. These exclude the very possibility, which the whole process was established by Yeats himself to explore, namely contact with a world outside all these fields which would come under the heading of 'religious, mystical, spiritual, magical'.

48   Ibid p 3.
49   Ibid p 118.
50   Ibid p 119.

Without at least countenancing such contact, there is little possibility of reconstructing 'the anterior thinking' of W.B. Yeats at whatever time or in whatever process he was engaged during most of his poetic life. In such a context as his, 'thinking' becomes a weak even though indispensable filter for wisdom from another source, and poetry establishes itself as the multifacetted container which alone can salvage from such depths the treasure which inspiration detects. The later poems of W.B. Yeats embody and transcribe the contours of such revelation.

In 1926 Yeats had written to Sturge Moore that 'what Whitehead calls the "three provincial centuries" are over. Wisdom and poetry return'. The two books of his poetry which probably best encompass these two life-giving realities are *The Tower* and *The Winding Stair*. And the two poems which set us, perhaps, upon the highest rock which W.B. Yeats was able to reach, are 'Sailing to Byzantium' and 'Byzantium'. He wrote in *A Vision*: 'I think if I could be given a month of antiquity and leave to spend it where I chose, I would spend it in Byzantium, a little before Justinian opened St Sophia and closed the Academy of Plato'.

In a BBC Broadcast, which he made in Belfast on the 8 September 1931, he elaborated:

> Now I am trying to write about the state of my soul, for it is right for an old man to make his soul, and some of my thoughts upon that subject I have put into a poem called 'Sailing to Byzantium'. When Irishmen were illuminating the Book of Kells [in the eighth century] and making the jewelled croziers in the National Museum, Byzantium was the centre of European civilisation and the source of its spiritual philosophy, so I symbolise the search for the spiritual life by a journey to that city.

I

That is no country for old men. The young
In one another's arms, birds in the trees,
Those dying generations – at their song,
The salmon-falls, the mackerel crowded seas,
Fish, flesh, or fowl, commend all summer long
Whatever is begotten born or dies.
Caught in that sensual music all neglect
Monuments of unageing intellect.

II

An aged man is but a paltry thing,
A tattered coat upon a stick, unless
Soul clap its hands and sing, and louder sing
For every tatter in its mortal dress,
Nor is there singing school but studying
Monuments of its own magnificence;
And therefore I have sailed the sees and come
To the holy city of Byzantium.

III

O sages standing in God's holy fire
As in the gold mosaic of a wall,
Come from the holy fire, perne in a gyre,
And be the singing-masters of my soul.
Consume my heart away; sick with desire
And fastened to a dying animal
It knows not what it is; and gather me
Into the artifice of eternity.

IV

Once out of nature I shall never take
My bodily form from any natural thing,
But such a form as Grecian goldsmiths make
Of hammered gold and gold enamelling
To keep a drowsy Emperor awake;
Or set upon a golden bough to sing
To lords and ladies of Byzantium
Of what is past, or passing, or to come.
(*W.B. Yeats, 'Sailing to Byzantium', 26 September, 1926*)

Resurrection of the body is the artifice of eternity which Yeats was trying to describe. Such resurrection out of time and into eternity is a spiral movement which requires of us, and in us, both the protection and the artificial structure of the tower along with the inner spiral movement of the winding stair, 'for that supreme art which is to win us from life and gather us into eternity like doves into their dove-cots'.[51]

The Winding Stair should be seen as combining with *The Tower* in the same way that both the physical building and its internal stairway eat into one another and form the composite image of interpenetrating gyres. The world of eternity transforms the nature of our material world by drilling into it, as a sculptor drills into stone to form a marble eye. The second book contains the poem *Byzantium*. Yeats was at one point going to make this the title of the book. Byzantium as an historical reality was the meeting place of two cultures that have formed the Western world. The whole city, with its great dome and its mosaics which defy nature and assert transcendence, and its theologically rooted and synthetic culture, can serve the poet as an image of the Heavenly City and the state of the soul when it is 'out of nature'.

....
51   W.B. Yeats, *Mythologies*, London MacMillan, 1959, p 301.

This was really, especially at this time in his life and after a recent illness, all that Yeats was now interested in. He writes in his diary for 1930: 'I am always, in all I do, driven to a moment which is the realisation of myself as unique and free, or to a moment which is the surrender to God of all that I am... could those two impulses, one as much a part of truth as the other, be reconciled, or if one or the other could prevail, all life would cease... Surely if either circuit, that which carries us into man or that which carries us into God, were reality, the generation had long since found its term'.[52] 'Sailing to Byzantium' is describing the first circuit, that which carries us into man. However 'Byzantium' attempts to describe the placement, the enactment, and the reality of the second circuit, that which carries us into God.

Denis Donoghue shows how Yeats's play *The Resurrection* battles with a similar theme and quotes the sentence spoken by the Greek student of Heracleitus in that play 'God and man die each other's life, live each other's death' as important commentary on the line in Byzantium which speaks of 'death-in-life and life-in-death'.[53] It is as if 'Sailing to Byzantium' was about the first part of that double spiral and 'Byzantium' about the second. Yeats tells us that the second poem was partly inspired by Sturge Moore's letter on the inadequacy of 'Sailing to Byzantium'. Moore was 'sceptical as to whether mere liberation from existence has any value or probability as a consummation. I prefer with Wittgenstein, whom I don't understand, to think that nothing at all can be said about ultimates, or reality in an ultimate sense... Your 'Sailing to Byzantium', magnificent as the first

....

52 Denis Donoghue, *We Irish*, University of California Press, 1986, p 78.
53 Donoghue quotes this passage to show that 'In prose-moments Yeats was prepared to concede, of Self or Soul, that one is as much a part of truth as the other, but in most of the poems he enlisted under one banner and for the time being served it zealously. In The Winding Stair, when it came to a choice between the circuit which carried him into man and that which carried him into God, he chose man; but even as he voted he felt the burden of misgiving, loss, sacrifice, waste. The longing expressed in the Diary points directly to "Byzantium" and *The Resurrection*' Ibid p 77.

three stanzas are, lets me down in the fourth, as such a goldsmith's bird is as much nature as a man's body, especially if it only sings like Homer or Shakespeare of what is past or passing or to come to Lords and Ladies'.[54]

Yeats sent him a copy of 'Byzantium' so that he might design the symbolic cover for his new book, *The Winding Stair*, saying that Moore's criticism was the origin of the poem because his objection 'showed me that the idea needed exposition'.[55]

Byzantium
The unpurged images of day recede;
The Emperor's drunken soldiery are abed;
Night resonance recedes, night-walkers' song
After great cathedral gong;
A starlit or a moonlit dome distains
All that man is,
All mere complexities,

The fury and the mire of human veins.
Before me floats an image, man or shade,
Shade more than man, more image than shade;
For Hades' bobbin bound in mummy-cloth
May unwind the winding path;
A mouth that has no moisture and no breath
Breathless mouths may summon;
I hail the superhuman;
I call it death-in-life and life-in-death.

Miracle, bird or golden handiwork,
More miracle than bird or handiwork,

54   W.B. *Yeats and T. Sturge Moore: Their Correspondence 1901-37*, ed. Ursula Bridge, New York: Oxford University Press, 1953, P 162.
55   Ibid p 164.

Planted on the starlit golden bough,
Can like the cocks of Hades crow,
Or, by the moon embittered, scorn aloud
In glory of changeless metal
Common bird or petal
And all complexities of mire or blood.

At midnight on the Emperor's pavement flit
Flames that no faggot feeds, nor steel has lit,
Nor storm disturbs, flames begotten of flame,
Where blood-begotten spirits come
And all complexities of fury leave,
Dying into dance,
An agony of trance,

An agony of flame that cannot singe a sleeve.
Astraddle on the dolphin's mire and blood,
Spirit after spirit! The smithies break the flood,
The golden smithies of the Emperor!
Marbles of the dancing floor
Break bitter furies of complexity,
Those images that yet
Fresh images beget,
That dolphin-torn, that gong-tormented sea.
(*W.B. Yeats, September 1930*)

In *The Tower*, Yeats made his home, Thoor Ballylee, an emblem of the imagination's constructive power. It is a symbol of the symbol. The book belongs to the first circuit. The second book, *The Winding Stair,* belongs to the second circuit and supplies the second gyre which is meant to move into the first and die with its life while it lives with its death. Imagination provides both circuits, but this is also because Imagination itself is the one human faculty which is capable of circumscribing both. W.B. Yeats and William Blake believed that

> this world of Imagination is the world of Eternity; it is the divine bosom into which we shall all go after the death of the Vegetated body. This World of Imagination is Infinite and Eternal, whereas the world of Generation, or Vegetation, is Finite and Temporal... The Human Imagination... appear'd to Me... throwing off the Temporal that the Eternal might be Establish'd.... In Eternity one Thing never Changes into another Thing. Each Identity is Eternal.[56]

Byzantium is an experiment in articulating the poet's own reality, or shape, or image, after he is transfigured by death. Each of the selected images initiate him and ourselves into the mysteries which death delivers. In his 1930 diary, Yeats wrote a prose draft:

> Subject for a poem. April 30th. Describe Byzantium as it is in the system towards the end of the first Christian millennium. A walking mummy. Flames at the street corners where the soul is purified, birds of hammered gold singing in the golden trees, in the harbour [dolphins], offering their backs to the wailing dead that they may carry them to Paradise. These subjects have been in my head for some time, especially the last.[57]

> The soul has a plastic power, and can after death, or during life, should the vehicle leave the body for a while, mould it to any shape it will by an act of imagination, though the more unlike to the habitual that shape is, the greater the effort.[58]

56 Quoted in Frank Kermode, *The Romantic Image*, London, 1957, p 89.
57 W.B. Yeats, *Explorations*, London, Macmillan, 1962, p 290.
58 W.B. Yeats, *Mythologies*, London MacMillan, 1959, p 349.

In *A Vision* Yeats wrote of Justinian's construction of Hagia Sophia (AD 560) as one of history's closest approximations to the
ahistorical beauty of the full moon, Phase 15 of the gyre: 'Byzantium
substituted for formal Roman magnificence, with its glorification of
physical power, an architecture that suggests the Sacred City in the
Apocalypse of St John'.

The characteristics of Byzantium are an almost complete dematerialisation, as if the city were manufactured out of air and shadowed
on water, a deliberate destruction of the boundary between life and
art – human beings are translated into mosaic, while symbols have
the presence of 'a perfect human body; the beatitude of dead souls
was realised there on earth'.

Resolution within the poem, as I read it, comes only in the last
line, even in the last image: 'that gong-tormented sea'. The poet
changes from the visual to the aural image.[59] Dematerialisation reaches its point zero on the dancing floor, without yet relinquishing its
essentially human and passionate bodily texture, by delivering itself
into rhythm, music, song. 'Song is existence', as Rilke has famously
written. Yeats's poetry is the psalmody which will endure and which
will persecute eternity. The gong has already appeared at midnight
in the cathedral and the gong was also the aural image Yeats used
for the affect which Maude Gonne exercised upon his earthly life.
Whatever his love for her has meant, this is the keening sound
which must linger into eternity if he is to survive his own mortali-
ty and perdure. Without the gong there is no remnant of passionate humanity. The gong is what secures everlasting remembrance
of things past, in the otherwise bland and undifferentiated ocean
of eternity.

59   This suggestion is somewhat less isolated and presumptuous in the light of recent
    research by Nóirín Ní Riain in her Doctorate thesis *Theosony: The Sound of God*,
    University of Limerick, 2003.

Eternity becomes 'gong-tormented' by 'a slow low note and an iron bell'. This was the way Yeats described the reverberation throughout his own life caused by his meeting with Maud Gonne [gone/gong] 'a sound as of a Burmese gong, an overpowering tumult'.[60] It is as if he has agreed with Sturge Moore that any attempt to immortalise the songbird by fixing it in gold enamelling in mosaic or statuery is unworkable. Nothing of that kind can endure. Transverberation of eternity can only occur through sound. This last image of the poem harks back to the second verse of 'Sailing to Byzantium' where 'An aged man is but a paltry thing' 'unless soul clap its hands and sing, and louder sing/ for every tatter in its mortal dress'. The five verses of Byzantium are coping with these 'tatters'. 'The unpurged images of day' have to wait for the second last line of the poem to beget fresh images which can release souls and the poem into eternity and infinity. The scenario of the poem takes place on the Emperor's pavement where 'complexities of mire and blood' achieve some purification and preparation for the journey to Paradise. But even the 'agony of flame' is work of each one's imagination 'but her own conscience made visible'[61] not a real flame that might 'singe a sleeve'.

There is a mosaic on the pavement which represents dolphins and the great sea. This is Byzantine art which, like the poem, is a mixture of Greek, Roman and Asian elements, all of which combine to allow the viewer to pass into another dimension, the divine, the infinite, the eternal. All the verses up to the last line are concerned with the circuit which carries us into man. There is an ominous presence beyond, another greater ocean, which surrounds the pavement and which can flood. But the five verses deal with purification, with the attempt to purge the images of day. Such rummaging in 'the foul rag and bone shop' produces 'a heap of broken images'. They are

60   *W.B. Yeats, The Poems,* edited by Daniel Albright, London: Dent, Everyman's
      Library, 1992; rev. edn 1994, Notes no 4 page 718.
61   Ibid Notes 27 Pp 719-720.

smashed on the marble dance floor until at the last moment as the ocean of infinity invades, they manage to beget fresh images which carry us into God. There are two fresh images, but these are enough to portray the new situation. It is as if this other reality in the background eventually overwhelms, and the human soul whose vehicle is the dolphin, tears open the ocean, before disgorging its reverberation into the deep. There is a sexual penetration of infinity implied in the image of the dolphin's dive. Each soul astride a dolphin's back returns to the deep with a reverberating resonance akin to that created in the soul of Yeats when he first met Maud Gonne. Eternity is torn and each penetration leaves its watermark. In drafts of the previous poem 'Sailing to Byzantium' there were dolphins in 'the foam/ Where the dark drowsy fins a moment rise/ Of fish, that carry souls to Paradise'. And it was originally a dolphin who would 'gather me/ Into the artifice of eternity'.[62] Yeats was clear also that each soul was carried by its own particular dolphin. Sturge Moore's original design for the cover of the book in which Byzantium appears had all humanity riding on the back of one huge dolphin. Yeats wrote to him: 'One dolphin, one man'.[63] The shockwave caused by the dolphin's dive allows our bodies and our breath to make the impact of a gong. Dolphins use sound frequencies of natural sonar [acronym, made up from the initial letters of _so_und _na_vigation (and) _r_anging] which emits ultrasound waves to localise things and communicate. Such acoustical oceanography is called 'echolocation'. A dolphin's signal frequencies can have an effect on the human brain by modifying brainwave activity. Their sonar language can travel hundreds of miles through the ocean.

62 W.B. Yeats, *The Poems,* edited by Daniel Albright, London: Dent, Everyman's Library, 1992; rev. edn 1994, Notes no 4 page 720.
63 *W.B. Yeats and T. Sturge Moore: Their Correspondence 1901-37,* ed. Ursula Bridge, New York: Oxford University Press, 1953, P 165.

Dying each other's death, living each other's life is here presented as a sinking into supernatural splendour, making a splash and a reverberation which infinity won't forget in a very long time, hopefully for eternity.

CHAPTER FIVE

○

Heaney as Hyphen

The kingdom of God is not something that can be observed,
nor will people say, 'Here it is', or 'There it is',
because the kingdom of God is in your midst.
(*Luke: 17: 20-21*)

Seamus Heaney was born in 1939, the year W.B. Yeats died. Whereas Yeats was our great poet of the Anglo-Irish tradition who polished
and burnished the 'Anglo' half of that equation, Heaney concentrated
his attention on the conjunction between the two words, between
the two worlds.[1]

Two buckets were easier carried than one.
I grew up in between.[2]

Heaney was the hyphen between Anglo-Irish, North-South,
Post-Modern, even, as he said himself, between Derry and Derrida.
The conjunction is one of the most prolific parts of speech in the Heaney oeuvre. Everything in his life and his work contributed to some
interconnection. His funeral cortege from Donnybrook in Dublin 4,

---

1   'I don't think that there is one true bearer of Irishness. There are different
    versions, different narratives, as we say, and you start out in possession of one of
    these. Maybe righteously in possession, as one of Yeats's Anglo-Irish, say,—"no
    petty people"—or as one of my own "big-voiced scullions". But surely you have
    to grow into an awareness of the others and attempt to find a way of imagining a
    whole thing. That really is the challenge, to open the definition and to make the
    domain of Irishness in Ireland—I hate to use the word *pluralist*, it's so prim and
    righteous—to make it open and available'. From the 1997 interview, The Art of
    Poetry No 75, *The Paris Review*, No 144, Fall 1997.
2   Seamus Heaney, *Opened Ground, Poems 1966-1996*, London, Faber, 1998, p. 295.

through the country to the family plot at Bellaghy, County Derry, in Northern Ireland, marked a moving hyphen graphically, between Ireland north and south. This is also the link he tried to forge for us in 'The Human Chain' whose end is peace.

His life was ambidextrous. Published in London by Faber and Faber, he taught at both Oxford and Harvard. He moved from Northern Ireland to live in Dublin and Wicklow. He was multi-lingual, international, a poet of the whole planet, bestriding the globe. He was not to be domesticated or appropriated by any particular cause.[3] Born on a farm in County Derry, he swapped a pen for a shovel and rewrote the script, wishing to preserve the best of all the worlds he had inhabited. As a poet he understood that each of us is responsible for our own posture in this shifting world. We can be given a wrong-headed version of that world when we are young. This can skew our position and falsify our alignment. We have to follow, he would suggest, with sensitivity and attention, the orthodoxy of our own humanity. While 'keeping an eye/ On the eye in the level/ Before the cement set',[4] we must assess critically the world-view we received in our youth. Heaney set out to examine the real world with his own compass, taking his own soundings, making assessments adequate to the truth he was registering on the sprockets of his sensibility. Such is the essential ethic of the poet. You also have to stand up for yourself and your stance has to be versatile and sturdy:[5]

....

3   'The reader to whom everything is directed, the one Mandelstam called "the reader in posterity", is as much for me a Northern Protestant as anything else. But listen to what I'm saying! Protestant, Catholic—the point is to fly under or out and beyond those radar systems. Ideally our work is directed towards some just, disinterested point of reception. A locus of justice, a kind of listening post and final appeal court. I regard many of the things I know and have to tell about as deriving from my Catholic minority background in Northern Ireland, but I don't regard that as a circumstance that determines my audience or my posture'. From the 1997 interview, The Art of Poetry No 75, The Paris Review, No 144, Fall 1997.
4   Seamus Heaney, District and Circle, London, Faber, 2006, p. 8.
5   Ibid, p. 5.

The way you had to stand to swing the sledge
Your two knees locked, your lower back shock-fast
As shields in a testudo, spine and waist
A pivot for the tight-braced, tilting rib-cage.

There was also a link to be made between the physical world and a world 'beyond' the merely physical, which is the etymology of 'metaphysics'. Heaney would 'forge' a connection between the world we experience around us and another world which he would have been brought up to call 'supernatural'. He would reject the presentation of such a world which his religion and his culture outlined as a dogmatic belief structure, and he would meticulously explore and redefine in his own words the possibility of such connection. His religion and his literary vocation were at odds in this domain, and one of his tasks was to come to terms with such antagonism.[6]

Station Island (1984) is an attempt to come to terms with the divide between literature and Catholicism in Ireland. The island of Lough Derg becomes a poetic fulcrum. The problem for the native poet is how to assert independence against the double tyrannies of a Catholic state and an anti-Catholic literary paradigm. Heaney is not satisfied with previous attempts to straddle this divide. He refuses to offer a print out of the prevailing prejudice. In such a judicious balancing act Czeslaw Milosz was something of a mentor. 'Like Catholic Poland over the course of the twentieth century's two great wars, the idea of the Irish nation presents a tight knot of moral, political, philosophical, religious, and aesthetic problems for the artist. *Station Island*

6   'I was wanting to write about contemporary Ireland, the Republic of Ireland, as a country with a religious subconscious but a secular destiny—at the point of transition from the communality of religious devotion to the loneliness of modernity and subjectivity. The community in the poem has lost the sense of its own destiny and of any metaphysical call'. Here Heaney is talking about his poem 'The Mud Vision' from the collection *The Haw Lantern* [1987] [cf. *Opened Ground, Poems 1966-1996*, London, Faber, 1998, p. 321] in the 1997 interview, The Art of Poetry No 75, *The Paris Review*, No 144, Fall 1997.

becomes Heaney's way of thoroughly examining his moral conduct, specifically in relation to the carnage of the recent, decades-long, still unresolved Northern Troubles'.[7]

Heaney had been given the opportunity to distance himself from the provincial, to experience the wider cosmopolitan perspective, and to come to terms with 'spirituality' in Ireland. 'One of the most persistent questions asked by 'Station Island', is whether Catholicism can ever be separated from nationalism in Ireland'. Can such a place as Station Island ever rid itself of 'the tribal taboo'? Is there a possibility that this shrine could return to a previous incarnation, 'separating religious Lough Derg from its iconic, political status'. The question posed by Heaney's interrogation is 'whether the shrine can ever be rescued from its role, its most recent reification in history, as the standard bearer of the extremely conservative Catholicism essential to De Valera's vision of Ireland?' Is there a wider, more open, less restrictive Catholicism than 'the Tridentine devotional-based, exercise-driven, mechanical version of the faith, which actually overtakes Ireland in the early nineteenth century and comes to eclipse the more ecstatic, experiential, and to some, superstitious character of the pilgrimage in earlier centuries. He also questions the degree to which this legalistic version of religion is implicated in a similarly obedient, knee-crooking form of nationalism. Heaney is pushed or guided towards an encounter with God which is not mediated through Irish Catholicism, but which happens without the need of any intermediary through direct mystical contact with the Divine, the possibility of achieving transcendence without having to employ any of the locally available transport systems. This poem could become something of a spiritual manifesto for us all, and Heaney could be 'a latter-day and revised Stephen Daedalus forging a conscience of rural Catholic Ireland – even more, of rural Catholic Northern Ireland'.[8]

7   Peggy O'Brien, *Writing Lough Derg*, Syracuse University Press, New York, 2006, p. xix.
8   Ibid. Pp. 168-9.

O'Brien believes that 'Heaney has been working for years towards making space for contemporary metaphysical poetry in the Irish literary tradition'. The fact that others fail to detect this dimension, and accuse those who suggest it as reading more into the poems than they contain, prompts this author to pursue her intuition even to interpretation of the pauses between the words, her reading between the lines:

> Indeed, the more spiritually trenchant Heaney's introspection becomes in his career, the more the silence beyond polyphony becomes his hermeneutic key. . . These gestational, nonverbal spaces have always been the potent heart of Heaney's poetry and perhaps his residual, not fully articulated faith.[9]

Poetry cannot achieve such a contemporary metaphysical space on its own. It has to be accompanied by a certain kind of critical understanding that is guarantor of its authenticity and exegete of its accomplishment. Such thought can facilitate the journey to and from the protectorate of poetry. Grappling irons and gang-planks are necessary for pedestrian access to such a treasure trove. O'Brien's book ferries us to and from the island in a way that makes pleas of invincible ignorance about this itinerary unconvincing. Ireland is now enjoying a new era of religious poetry, she affirms. 'By "religious" I emphatically do not mean Catholic, nor do I refer to any orthodoxy'. Her detailed and intuitive study shows that

> the Lough Derg poetry is as close to prayer as it is possible for words to come while still retaining reason and avoiding the rote... This tradition of writings, in a sense religious *Dindshenchas*,[10] provides a neutral

---

9   Ibid Pp 196-197.
10   The *dindsenchas* [meaning "lore of places"] comprise about 176 poems plus a number of prose commentaries and prose tales from early Irish literature, recounting the origins of place-names and traditions concerning events and characters associated with the places in question.

but formal zone where the individual's innate spirituality can express itself without crooking the knee to Church or nation.[11]

The metaphysics to which Heaney's poetry introduces us is not 'beyond' [as the word 'meta' means in Greek] the physical world in which we live; it is a dimension of that very world itself. Nor is it 'above' the natural world as words such as 'supernatural' might imply. It may not be readily visible to us who live so avidly and one-dimensionally in this world, but that does not mean that it is not situated squarely within. Heaney, as one of the great poets of the natural world, repudiates any such layering of experience. There is another reality but it is within this one in which we live. Our connection with this other reality is not the fervent mystical bond with Nature which allowed the Romantic movement to see earth as a glossy surface with Wordsworth on his skates scoring sheet music several inches above the ground: 'As he flashed from the clutch of earth along its curve and left/ it scored the whet and scud of steel on placid ice'.[12] Heaney does not skate some inches above the icy surface of the earth. He, like the ground hog, surfaces through the topsoil barely distinguishable from the mud, the dirt, the soil, from which he has been dredged. Poetically speaking, Heaney identifies more with Kavanagh[13] in the Irish tradition and with Hardy[14] in the English.

....

11   Ibid p. 262.
12   Seamus Heaney, *District and Circle*, London, Faber, 2006, p. 22.
13   'I was sort of pupped out of Kavanagh. I read him in 1962, after I'd graduated from Queen's and was teaching at St Thomas's, where my headmaster was the short-story writer Michael McLaverty. He lent me Kavanagh's *Soul for Sale*, which includes 'The Great Hunger', and at that moment the veil of the study was rent: it gave me this terrific breakthrough from English literature into home ground'. From the 1997 interview, The Art of Poetry No 75, *The Paris Review*, No 144, Fall 1997.
14   From the moment I read 'The Oxen', the moment I read the opening chapters of *Return of the Native*, I was at home with him—something about the vestigial ballad atmosphere, the intimacy, the oldness behind and inside the words, the peering and puzzlement and solitude. He was there like a familiar spirit from school days. I remember hearing the poem 'Weathers' read on the BBC radio when I was eleven or twelve and never forgetting it. 'The Oxen' I learned by heart around that time also. I loved the oddity and previousness of the English in it. "The lonely barton by yonder coomb" —that can still make me feel sad and taken care of all at once, *le cor au fond du bois* with a local accent'. Ibid.

What the poet has to do to create such music is to let his ear attend to 'where the extravagant / Passed once under full sail into the longed-for'.[15] This attention and concentration from the hub to the circumference, the centre to the rim, is personified in an anecdote about Thomas Hardy who lay down flat on the earth allowing his 'small cool brow' to experiment with infinity by making it 'like an anvil waiting for sky to make it sing the perfect pitch of his dumb being'. And this note having been sounded would echo above 'the resonating amphorae' to create ripples of sound-waves on the ether which would last and be lasting for earth:

> Outward from there, to be the same ripple
> Inside him at its last circumference.[16]

Such poems are about where human being stands in the cosmos, the human being who has recognised that we need to go underground to find roots. 'Cattle out in the rain, their knowledgeable/ Solid standing and readiness to wait,/ These I learned from'.[17]

Heaney introduces us to a 'double vision', which detects in the visible traces of the invisible. To achieve this optic we must close down our 'normal' 'ordinary' 'commonsense' way of viewing the world around us, and allow the poet to provide us with the 3D goggles, as it were, which can supply a depth charge of the unfathomable to certain images. What poets can accomplish actively through their poetic work each one of us can achieve passively through their [in] tuition.

....

15   Seamus Heaney, *Opened Ground, Poems 1966-1996*, London, Faber, 1998, p. 390
16   Ibid. p. 362.
17   Seamus Heaney, *District and Circle*, London, Faber, 2006, p 57.

Especially in his 1991 volume, *Seeing Things*, Heaney shows us, on his 'journey back/ into the heartland of the ordinary',[18] particular realities in our world which act as portals to the unknown, windows on the invisible, doorways into the dark, 'a half-door/ opening directly into starlight'.[19] The poems place us in situations that allow this privileged vision. In 'Field of Vision' the woman sat for years looking out the window:[20]

> I remember this woman who sat for years
> In a wheelchair, looking straight ahead
> Out the window at sycamore trees unleafing
> And leafing at the far end of the lane.
>
> Face to face with her was an education
> Of the sort you got across a well-braced gate
> One of those lean, clean, iron, roadside ones
> Between two whitewashed pillars, where you could see
>
> Deeper into the country than you expected
> And discovered that the field behind the hedge
> Grew more distinctly strange as you kept standing
> Focused and drawn in by what barred the way.

The gate between whitewashed pillars is the opening through which 'you could see/ deeper into the country than you expected' and what you saw beyond grew 'more distinctly strange' as you were drawn into it 'by what barred the way'.

---

18 Seamus Heaney, *Seeing Things*, London, Faber, 1991, p. 7. This poem 'The Journey back' was not included in Seamus Heaney, *Opened Ground, Poems 1966-1996*, London, Faber, 1998.
19 Seamus Heaney, *Opened Ground, Poems 1966-1996*, London, Faber, 1998, p. 384.
20 Ibid. p. 343.

'The Skylight' allowed 'extravagant sky' to enter the claustrophobic roof space 'and held surprise wide open',[21] 'freshening your outlook/ beyond the range you thought you'd settled for'.[22] The poet is teaching us 'to be on the *qui vive*, weaving and dodging'[23] until 'the visible sea at a distance from the shore' was turned into 'a lambent troop that exercised/ on the borders of your vision' and 'had withdrawn/ behind the skyline to manoeuvre and regroup'.[24] In the triptych of the titular poem 'Seeing Things' we are introduced to the Latin word for this poetic work: *Claritas*, which 'is perfect' as a translation of the 'bright sunlight' which allows us to see 'in that utter visibility' that 'the stone's alive with what's invisible'.[25] The new metaphysics is the earth alive with what's invisible. We are introduced to the invisible within the visible.

On the night Seamus Heaney was buried, RTÉ Radio played his version of *The Burial at Thebes*. There were parallels. *Antigone*, the fifth century BCE tragedy by Sophocles on which Heaney's play is based, concerns the titular daughter of Oedipus, King of Thebes, in Greece. She learns that her two brothers Polyneices and Etocles have killed each other fighting on different sides of a war. Creon, Antigone's uncle and the newly appointed King of Thebes, buries Etocles, who fought on the Theban side, hailing him as a great hero. He refuses to bury Polyneices, because he was a 'traitor' fighting on the opposite side. Anyone who attempts to defy this order will die.

Antigone, engaged to be married to Haemon, Creon's son, defies this order and buries her dead brother. She is sealed in a tomb and left to die. Fighting the wrong battle or the wrong war can lead, in any century or circumstance, to excommunication. Heaney advocates sympathy for both causes: 'The end of art is peace.' Peace requires

21   Ibid. p 350.
22   Ibid. p. 383.
23   Ibid. p. 387.
24   Ibid. p. 391.
25   Ibid. p. 339-340.

love of the conjunction, the hyphen between the ones at war. Heaney wants to move us all out of tiny parochialism towards mid-Atlantic where cosmopolitan culture can spawn. As Hughie O'Donoghue has said in an interview: 'I have always been focused on what I would see as cultural rather than national identity. Culture is about sharing; nationalism is about ownership'.[26]

But how can we hope to understand the mindset of Antigone seven thousand years ago? Tradition can only manifest itself in objects still remaining in our world. Gadamer puts it well: 'It is the general nature of tradition that only that of the past which is preserved offers the possibility of historical knowledge'.[27] We can only recreate our past from whatever still remains extant in our world at present. Books, music, theatre, paintings are great carriers of what we can never experience personally, but most of what we can sense about the lives of our predecessors is conveyed by strange and durable remnants left lying around in our world, but which might also carry some secret message for us if we were up to interpreting it.

The Tollund Man, discovered in Denmark in 1950, is probably the best preserved remains of someone who lived in the fourth century BCE. Those who discovered him in 1950 thought they had found evidence of a recent murder. Experts have deduced from these remains that he must have been in his forties or fifties when he died; that he was hanged either as a traitor or as a sacrifice to gods. His fate was similar to Antigone's and his burial place, unlike hers, was under two metres of bogland. The chemistry of such a graveyard caused the body to be naturally mummified. The corpse looks as if it were buried recently. Much is made, in some commentaries, about Heaney's interest in, and poems about, this man on display in a Danish museum. Parallels are drawn between sacrificial victims in Jutland and

26   Interview with Hughie O'Donoghue by Brian McAvera, *Irish Arts Review*, Autumn [September-November, 2013] p 75.
27   Hans-Georg Gadamer, *Truth and Method*, London, Sheed & Ward, 1975, p. 257.

Northern Ireland.[28] But however true such implications may or may not be, it is also true to say that Heaney was himself led on a journey by that ancient corpse who taught him that '[t]he soul exceeds its circumstances Yes./ History not to be granted the last word/ Or the first claim'.[29] There is no way that someone standing in a museum six centuries later, studying this remnant, can ever hope to give an adequate assessment of its culture or circumstances.

Poetically speaking, after a lifetime of obsession with bog land, and forty years of struggle with the bog bodies, by the age of sixty-eight, Heaney becomes his own 'Tollund man in springtime'. In a letter to me from hospital in Donnybrook after his stroke, Heaney writes [15 September, 2006]: 'Nobody has seen the story behind the Tollund Man fable so thoroughly, nobody has amplified the signals so amply'.

So, let us try to amplify the signals even more amply. In a series of six sonnets Heaney describes how 'on the sixth day' he, as the Tollund Man, 'got lifted up' out of the bog 'brown and bare',[30] lifted into the display case on the international stage especially by Nobel laureate status: 'the plain mysteriousness/ of your sheeted self inside that neck-tied cope/ Half sleeveless surplice, half hoodless Ku

---

28 'I see the Bog Poems in Pinsky's terms as an answer. They were a kind of holding action. They were indeed a bit like the line drawn in the sand. Not quite an equivalent for what was happening, more an attempt to rhyme the contemporary with the archaic. 'The Tollund Man', for example, is the first of the Bog Poems I wrote. Essentially, it is a prayer that the bodies of people killed in various actions and atrocities in modern Ireland, in the teens and twenties of the century as well as in the more recent past, a prayer that something would come of them, some kind of new peace or resolution. In the understanding of his Iron Age contemporaries, the sacrificed body of Tollund Man germinated into spring, so the poem wants a similar flowering to come from the violence in the present. Of course it recognizes that this probably won't happen, but the middle section of the poem is still a prayer that it should. The Bog Poems were defenses against the encroachment of the times, I suppose'. From the 1997 interview, The Art of Poetry No 75, *The Paris Review*, No 144, Fall 1997.

29 *District and Circle*, Faber, 2006, p 56

30 Ibid. p. 55.

Klux cape'.[31] This last about having a haircut as a child in an elaborate swivel-chair of a barber's shop. The imagery contains temptations towards using such pedestals to become an authoritarian bishop or a sectarian murderer. The word 'cope' derives from the Latin *caput* meaning 'head', the same root as 'cape' or 'cap'. Such emblematic garments, such 'overalls', symbolise, in these images, priestly dignity and purity; 'surplice', the second image, is an 'angelic' white garment used sometimes by choirs to give the effect of wings and derives from *superpellicium*, over one's *pellis* meaning 'skin'. It was probably simply a respectably clean item worn for worship over grubby clothes. However, with Heaney, we have to discard any such angelic garb and wear an altogether more earthy 'helmet' to plumb the depths of contemporary shamanism.

The metaphysical poet of the twenty-first century has to work from the ground up. Heaney's task as a poet is somehow to go down into this element and either haul something up out of it, or allow it to 'foster a heavy greenness'[32] in himself. He 'panicked at the shiftiness and heft of the craft itself'.[33] And 'craft' here can be understood as both boat and work of the artist. The kind of openness required of the poet goes down into the water and allows the water to use it as a filter or a sponge. It is an openness also to the earth, a way of dwelling in the earth, of designing a house, open through the floor to the bare earth, open through windows and the roof to total exposure:

> I was four but I turned four hundred maybe
> Encountering the ancient dampish feel
> Of a clay floor ...
> Ground of being. Body's deep obedience

---

31   Ibid. p 34.
32   A quotation from John Montague introducing the poem 'Fosterling' in Seamus Heaney, *Opened Ground, Poems 1966-1996*, London, Faber, 1998, p. 357.
33   Ibid. p. 339.

To all its shifting tenses ...
Out of that earth house I inherited ...[34]

By the true act and art of poetry a journey is made which allows earth to be inhabited and space to be recapitulated. Who could blame any poet tempted to 'roof it again. Batten down. Dig in'[35] rather than stand 'unroofed and obvious'[36] saying '[a] farewell to surefooted-ness' by awaiting 'a pitch beyond our usual hold upon ourselves'.[37] Such is the torture of allowing oneself to be drawn by language, as Hector was dragged around the walls of Troy.

The open they came into by these moves
Stood opener, hopes came off the world.[38]

Poem *viii* of 'Lightenings' tells how the monks of Clonmacnoise were at prayer inside the oratory when a ship passing in the air above them got its anchor hooked into the altar rails. 'A crewman shinned and grappled down the rope'. He could not release the anchor.
'This man can't bear our life here and will drown',
The abbot said, 'unless we help him'. So
They did, the freed ship sailed, and the man climbed back
Out of the marvellous as he had known it.[39]

Heaney and the poetry 'sluggish in the doldrums of what happens' have to be tempted into the marvellous as he has not known it –

34   Ibid. p. 384.
35   Ibid. p. 359.
36   Seamus Heaney, *Seeing Things*, London, Faber, 1991, p. 12. This poem 'A Haul' was not included in Seamus Heaney, *Opened Ground, Poems 1966-1996*, London, Faber, 1998.
37   Seamus Heaney, *Seeing Things*, London, Faber, 1991, p. 86. This poem xxviii of 'Crossings' was not included in Seamus Heaney, *Opened Ground, Poems 1966-1996*, London, Faber, 1998.
38   Seamus Heaney, *Opened Ground, Poems 1966-1996*, London, Faber, 1998, p. 376.
39   Ibid. p. 364.

'Me waiting until I was nearly fifty / to credit marvels ... Time to be dazzled and the heart to lighten'.[40] Heaney himself says about the Clonmacnoise poem:

> I take it to be pure story. It has the entrancement of a narrative that's mysterious and absolute. It needs no explanation but even so, you could read it as a text about the necessity of being in two places at the one time, on the ground with the fatherly earthiness, but also keeping your mind open and being able to go up with the kite, on the magic carpet too, and live in the world of fantasy. To live in either world entirely and resolutely, and not to shift, is risky. For your wholeness you need to inhabit both worlds. I think the medieval notion of human beings occupying the angelic situation between the angels and the beasts is true. When I wrote *Seeing Things*, I think I had been quite close to the ground, and that then I lifted up my eyes to the hills, to the roof and to the Clonmacnoise boat.[41]

Earlier 'The Forge' made an anvil out of the hyphen, describing it as an altar, 'set there immoveable' on which real iron can be beaten out.[42] And hyphens abound in many of the poems such as 'St Kevin and the Blackbird' which uses no less than eight of the 'and' conjunctions [acting as 'hyphens'] to string itself together. One of these hyphens is metaphysical because it allows the saint, the poet, and the reader to achieve important access: 'and, finding himself linked/ Into the network of eternal life'.[43]

The whole 2006 volume of poems, *District and Circle*, is further elaboration of such alternative metaphysics. 'Circling his own dis-

40 Ibid. p. 357.
41 *Reading the Future, Irish Writers in Conversation with Mike Murphy*, Lilliput Press, Dublin, 2000, p 90.
42 'The Forge' *Opened Ground*, op. cit. p. 19.
43 'St Kevin and the Blackbird' *Opened Ground*, p. 410.

trict' Heaney is undertaking an archaeological dig on behalf of humanity. This turns out to be, not just the familiar London tube line, but the underground transport system for a new metaphysics. Truth is here being unearthed by the most accomplished digger. Has he not received a Nobel prize for digging? 'Seamus, make me a side-arm to take on the earth/ A suitable tool for digging and grubbing the ground'.[44] The result is freshly mined, original, unalloyed truth. And this truth is also Heaney himself being dug up: 'a spade-plate slid and soughed and plied/ At my buried ear, and the levered sod/ Got lifted up'. The 'buried ear' is unearthed and primed to listen. This is the original meaning of humility, an ear fashioned from the earth [*humus* being the Latin word for earth].

There is an underground continent hidden from most citizens of the universe until discoveries were made at the beginning of the last century. Such discoveries require a new cartography adjusted to the map of humanity now unveiled. Hence the need for the new underground map of *District and Circle*. Philosophy to date has been an explanation of the universe and our position in it, from the perspective of human consciousness. Revelation of an unconscious area underpinning this carefully mapped scenario spells its redundancy, its incapacity to cope with the real situation which pertains. New methods, new approaches are necessary. We are beginning to realise that this unconscious quagmire can be logged into by an art which lures us to the borders of impenetrability. Something akin to a psychic earthquake has occurred causing the dislocation of our centre of gravity:

> The centre of the total personality no longer coincides with the ego, but with a point midway between the conscious and the unconscious. This would be the point of a new equilibrium, a

---

44 *District and Circle*, Faber, 2006, p 25.

new centring of the total personality, a virtual centre which, on account of its focal position between conscious and unconscious ensures for the personality a new and more solid foundation.[45]

When a horse is required to perform the somewhat unnatural task of jumping a fence its centre of gravity moves into the area of its neck. This explains why jockeys lean forward over the horse's neck when jumping. A somewhat similar shift of balance has been caused by recent discoveries about the shape of human being. The ground is moving and we are moving with it. Hurtling 'through galleried earth', as Heaney describes our voyage through such underground systems, standing up is as difficult as finding one's feet on an overcrowded tube train.

> Stepping on to it across the gap,
> On to the carriage metal, I reached to grab
> The stubby black roof-wort and take my stand.
> From planted ball of heel to heel of hand
> A sweet traction and heavy down-slump stayed me.

Such is the new 'stance' to be adopted if we are to achieve alignment with the centre of gravity astride both worlds. '... [T]hen a long centrifugal/ Haulage of speed through every dragging socket'.[46] The old stability of *terra firma* vanishes as we negotiate the swaying gangway. This marshy place, this bog, has been the focus of Heaney's poetic work and as John Burnside suggests:[47] 'the *original* artist finds a source, a well spring, and spends a lifetime attuning himself to

---

45 C.G.Jung, 'The Relations between the Ego and the Unconscious' *Collected Works*, Vol. 7, Two Essays on Analytical Psychology (Bollingen Series XX, 1966) p. 221.
46 *District and Circle*, Faber, 2006, p. 19.
47 *The Scotsman*, Saturday April 1, 2006

its dark, underground current'. How do we too achieve our balance along this new centre of gravity?

Heaney is developing an alphabet and a vocabulary to help us adapt to 'being in depth': the call to be astride the abyss between conscious and unconscious awareness. In most languages, especially the romance languages, the copula which represents 'being' is linked with the notion of standing. The verb 'to be' came long after recognition that I am standing here and you are standing there:

> Bearings taken, markings, cardinal points,
> Options, obstinacies, dug heels and distance
> Here and there and now and then, a stance.[48]

Being, as an ontological and philosophical concept, is based upon the experience of stability and rest, a stance taken. Such considerations pervade this entire book of poems:[49] 'The way you had to stand' [5], 'the shaft to be socketed in dead true and dead straight' [25], 'Spot-rooted' [18], 'on the spot' [54], 'I take my stand in front of my house of life'[76]. 'Here we're like sentries' [73]. He 'stood off,/ Bulrush, head in air, far from its lough' [57]. These poems are like standing stones 'after the fire' 'to make them realize what had stood so [16]'.

So much for 'being' as 'standing'. Becoming, on the other hand, is based upon the perception of motion, of coming and going. Language, like poetry, surprises these realities in their primary emergence and finds the words to usher them into consciousness. Later they are circumscribed with a whole vocabulary of technical metaphysics. District, in this collection, is your place of rest. It comes from the Latin *distringere* which means delineating or marking off. It describes a territory divided or defined for whatever purposes, usually a jurisdiction for administration. Circle adds the movement,

---

48   *District and Circle*, Faber, 2006, p 12.
49   Ibid. I give the page number in brackets after each of the quotations in the following paragraphs.

the 'corona of gold' [65]. The human stance has to be versatile and sturdy, 'any forwardness was unwelcome and bodies blindsided to themselves and other bodies' [18].

Can spirituality be embraced, the religious impulse affirmed, apart from the over-defining structure of a church? This was Heaney's question about Catholicism.[50] Can the experience of faith, indeed even the liberating sensation of transcendence, be freed from autocratic dogmatism? Heaney knew the personal experience of mysticism: 'call it the flight of the soul or the spirit. It helped me to lose my shyness of the vocabulary of eternity', he says in an interview about *District and Circle*.

Sweeney Astray (1983) was Heaney's first spiritual manifesto. In this sequence of poems he discovers within himself a source of freedom, his ability to fly. His spiritual quest was the overcoming through poetry of a form of cultural incarceration, trying to break free and make space for contemporary metaphysics. Poetry could provide the Credo for such resurrection. The title of his Nobel Lecture in 1995 was 'Crediting Poetry'.[51] He looked for a relationship with God where the individual's innate spirituality can express itself without crooking the knee to church or nation, he said in 1991.[52]

One of his more explicitly metaphysical surveys is the last poem in the 1996 collection *Spirit Level*:

....

50   'To be in the presence of a death is to be in the presence of something utterly simple and utterly mysterious. In my case, the experience restored the right to use words like *soul* and *spirit*, words I had become unduly shy of, a literary shyness, I suppose, deriving from a misplaced obedience to proscriptions of the abstract, but also a shyness derived from a complicated relationship with my own Catholic past. In many ways I love it and have never quite left it, and in other ways I suspect it for having given me such ready access to a compensatory supernatural vocabulary. But experiencing my parents' deaths restored some of the verity to that vocabulary. These words, I realized, aren't obfuscation. They have to do with the spirit of life that is within us'. From the 1997 interview, The Art of Poetry No 75, *The Paris Review*, No 144, Fall 1997.
51   The lecture is printed in *Opened Ground*, Pp. 447-467.
52   Seamus Heaney interviewed by Ian Hargreaves in *the Financial Times*, 10 June, 1991.

Postscript
And some time make the time to drive out west
Into County Clare, along the Flaggy Shore,
In September or October, when the wind
And the light are working off each other
So that the ocean on one side is wild
With foam and glitter, and inland among stones
The surface of a slate-grey lake is lit
By the earthed lightning of a flock of swans,
Their feathers roughed and ruffling, white on white,
Their fully-grown headstrong-looking heads
Tucked or cresting or busy underwater.
Useless to think you'll park of capture it
More thoroughly. You are neither here nor there,
A hurry through which known and strange things pass
As big soft buffetings come at the car sideways
And catch the heart off guard and blow it open.[53]

Here Heaney shows us the place inside ourselves from which the 'double vision' becomes possible. It is not enough to describe how to look at certain objects until, under his guidance, we can see that they are symbols of something other; it is more important to explain how to reach that place from which such perspectives become habitual. Each of us can excavate that cave at the back of our minds, the cave of the heart.

'Some time make the time to drive out west'. Each one of us should make this journey at a certain time, or at certain times, in our lives. Of course, for the poet there is a particular hinterland which makes up the actual geography of his image. The Flaggy Shore is on the coastline in Co. Clare, where the flat stone of the Burren meets

---

53   *Opened Ground*, p. 444.

the sea as it extends into the waters of Galway Bay. A paved second-
ary road runs along most of this shoreline made up of limestone
flags and rounded boulders. If you travel about a mile down this road
you come to the actual spot where Heaney must have parked (even
though he advises his readers not to do so!). The journey itself may
help find the inner sanctum of the poem's inspiration, but such a
physical and geographical step tracing is not necessary, for the place
to which the poet is pointing is an interior epistemological space
which any human being can reach, and from which we can experience a very particular kind of knowing.

The road is placed on a narrow ridge between the stony shoreline
and green fields which skirt the rocky hillside of the Burren. At a
particular bend in the road you come to an apex, which allows you
to look back and see on one side of the road over which you have
just traveled, the great ocean waves, and on the other, a long and
extended slate-grey pond, mirroring the surrounding rockiness. This
is a calm fresh water lake nearly always home to flocks of swans. The
swans are 'busy underwater'. They do not have the vision that you
have from the vantage-point, the privileged sentinel, where you can
see both the ocean and the land. The swans with their 'fully-grown
headstrong-looking heads' represent the acme of natural understanding. Some keep their head stuck inside their own feathers while
others basking in the glory of their self-assured magnificence are
'cresting'. Nature and natural intelligence are unaware [busy under
water] of the alternative view, especially when they at their most perspicacious and self-absorbed.

But you are not like that. 'You are neither here nor there'. You are
somewhere beyond or between. 'Here' is the world of practicality,
'a slate-grey lake' which is 'lit by the earthed lightning' of these particular intelligences, these 'fully-grown headstrong-looking heads'
that know it all. These heads are subject to what Heaney calls in a

different context 'the gravitational pull of the actual'.[54] Perception is not simply an assault on the senses. Perception is a creative act of imagination, not simply a mirror but rather a lamp which lights up the world. We see, as Blake put it, 'not with but through the eye'. This double vision is a way of seeing and feeling at the same time. It involves the heart as much as the head.

For the last two hundred years we have cultivated, privileged, and educated to the point of exacerbation one particular function of the brain which concerns mostly the neo-cortex, the third most recently developed area of our heads. But there is an alternative way of understanding the world which combines more effectively the whole interconnecting trilogy of our brain-space. Poets and artists have stumbled upon this alternative viewing-point, swimming against the massive current which channels the waterway in the other direction.

This is not just because humankind is 'blessed' with an 'awareness' to which the animal world is blind. No, at the root of our soul there is a place which makes us a different kind of being from the animals, and makes of our world a different kind of space. 'You are neither here nor there/ A hurry through which known and strange things pass'. The swans on the lake are calm. We are 'a hurry' full of familiar and unusual thoughts.

At this place at the apex of the soul, a sharp immortal diamond pierces through the patch-work of the world. Heaney represents 'there' by 'the ocean' 'wild with foam and glitter'. This presence 'on one side' opposite the place 'inland among stones' is 'without'; it is an absence. The draft from its opening casts a chill on the cosiness within. This opening onto the ocean is the other side of our life.

Our task as humans in the world is to achieve the balance between the clustering pull of the earth and the suctioning vortex of the abyss, as you might wave your arms to regain balance on a tot-

----

54 Seamus Heaney, *Finders Keepers: Selected Prose, 1971-2001*, Faber, 2002, p. 259.

tering wall or a fence. This space is 'neither here nor there', it is in between the within and the without.

Nor can we shut it out altogether as can the swans. Every shutter holds it in its curve. It is always there *in absentia*. Its mode of presence is absence so that no amount of walling up can seal it off. It haunts us even when 'inland among stones'. It is a modality of being which is not useful in any recognized commercial sense and yet it leads us beyond the paralysis of everyday existence. It is as if there are two ways of being in the world, one convex, the other concave. In the second we prepare ourselves to enter the world in a despoliative posture, crouched and ready to spring. In the first we take up an almost opposite stance, which allows us to see the world from down under. Such a posture reveals a kind of willing, an attitude towards the world, other than the greedy will to possession and power. This happens if we are prepared to relinquish the 'covetous vision' of things, which we find natural, and adopt the 'double vision' which, when we 'make the time to drive out west', not only allows us to see 'on one side' the ocean and 'inland among stones/ the surface of a slate-grey lake', but also this particular place allows us to change register so that our vision is not just that of our 'fully-grown headstrong-looking heads' but 'a work of the heart' as much as of the eyes.

Where is the 'space' and when is the 'time' of the convex world? By a movement of interiority, by sometime 'making the time' to drive out west, to places that are the edges of our normal everyday selves, we arrive at 'the flaggy shore'. The poet speaks from this innermost interiority, and the poetry, or what the poet says, speaks not only from both realms, but from the oneness of the two realised in himself. It is this place of 'the oneness of the two' that Heaney is picturing for us in a particular geographical location in County Clare. Reaching this spot is an epistemological breakthrough which stretches all our received wisdom in Western European Philosophy to breaking point. We reach the vanishing point where the tangent hits the circle. Medieval metaphysics would have described it as 'participation'. More recent philosophy is less garrulous and denies our capacity either to observe or to name it.

The poet who says more is the one who dwells in that place within, [the flaggy shore], which is in contact with this reality, and so allows the breath of both to be caught on the sprocket of each word and thus secrete into our culture a luminosity or phosphorescence which coats the poem as it emerges with the tang and fragrance of an invisibility. Great poets dwell in the secret places of the earth and their essential heartwork is production of honey from these rocks. Their poetry is language drenched in the moisture of the beyond. But whenever we have a sense experience, whenever we touch something, smell something, hear something, see something, we always, and at the same time, have a secret experience of this at another level. There is always this delicate shimmering gossamer around every experience which we, in our day to day commerce, our rush through the business schedule, fail to notice and invariably ignore. This second level experience, which is not something added like a coating or an undercarriage, but is something 'present' in its reticent presentation of the thing to our notice, is something we have to reactivate and examine. 'Useless to think you'll park or capture it/ more thoroughly'. It is almost as if we had to go back into the dark room of our experience and develop its implications from the negatives of the day-to-day photo call. That is why this poem is a 'postscript', it is written after the event 'in that serene and blessed mood' which Wordsworth describes in Tintern Abbey': 'with an eye made quiet by the power/ Of harmony, and the deep power of joy,/ We see into the life of things'.

Because this second level experience transcends our sense experience, we have to invent nets that can collect this phosphorescence, entrap this fragrance. In our ordinary day-to-day contact with reality this fine dust disperses itself and gets lost in the process of harvesting. It is not the content of what we glean from this harvest that gives us access, nor is it the ideas we contain in our heads. It is the contact, the meeting with reality that creates those sparks which we need to recover, if we are to have any inkling of the real meaning, the ontological weight of those same experiences. This is what essential poetry tries to do.

If we are to move forward towards a development which respects all the elements in the amalgam which we are, which we have become, which we hope to direct towards the most optimistic future, it is essential that we collaborate with scientists and artists who have the antennae and are the diviners, the creators, of our future. They are our eyes, our ears, our imaginations. Heaney put it this way in 1991:[55] 'My language and my sensibility is yearning to admit a kind of religious or transcendental dimension. But then there's the reality ... the complacency and the utter simplification of these things into social instructions. That's what's disappointing'. Artists shake our complacency and refuse 'the utter simplification of "these things" into social instructions'. One of the tasks of poetry, Heaney reminded us in his T.S. Eliot Memorial Lectures of 1986, is to resist moral cowardice. He uses examples of poets in those communist states in Eastern Europe who, until quite recently, were living in situations where art was either harnessed to government policy or else became a public enemy of state legislature and ideology. But most of us can recognize the world he is describing:[56]

> A world where poetry is required to take a position that is secondary to religious truth or state security or public order... In ideal republics, Soviet republics, in the Vatican and Bible-belt, it is common expectation that the writer will sign over

---

55 Seamus Heaney interviewed by Ian Hargreaves in *the Financial Times*, 10 June, 1991.
56 Seamus Heaney, *The Government of the Tongue*, London: Faber & Faber, 1988, p 96.

his or her individual, venturesome and potentially disruptive activity into the keeping of an official doctrine, a traditional system, a party line.

Nor do we have to be governed by a bloody dictator to undergo such doctrinaire browbeating. 'I am thinking, he says, not so much of authoritarian censorship as of an implacable consensus'. The role of the poet is to expose 'to the majority the abjectness of their collapse, as they flee for security into whatever self-deceptions the party line requires of them'. Like Cezanne at the beginning of the century, Heaney has been trying to show us how to see, how to 'credit marvels'. His poetry and his criticism should become an essential part of the probing which determines the direction we now want to take. Artists are like scouts in the evolutionary march. Their work is to explore the territory ahead and advise on the paths to be tested.

Nobody knew, and nobody better expressed 'the marvellous' of our life here on earth as did Seamus Heaney. 'Often when I'm on my own in the car, driving down from Dublin to Wicklow in spring or early summer – or indeed at any time of the year – I get this sudden joy from the sheer fact of the mountains to my right and the sea to my left, the flow of the farmland, the sweep of the road, the lift of the sky. There's a double sensation of here-and-nowness in the familiar place and far-and-awayness in something immense'.[57] The double sensation does justice to two worlds: the everyday world we see around us and the hidden world of mystery. 'Poetry represents the need for an ultimate court of appeal. The infinite spaces may be silent, but the human response is to say that this is not good enough, that there has to be more to it than neuter absence'.[58]

57   Dennis O'Driscoll, *Stepping Stones, Interviews with Seamus Heaney*, London, Faber, 2008, p 475.
58   Ibid. Pp 470-1.

You are neither here nor there,
A hurry through which known and strange things pass
As big soft buffetings come at the car sideways
And catch the heart off guard and blow it open.

Was Heaney an Irish Catholic, people ask. The question could be re-versed: did we know what to be 'Catholic' meant until we had followed his journey and ransacked his word hoard? Seamus Heaney was a man of his word. More prophet than priest, the Word was mediator between heaven and earth, not any preordained code or prescribed ritual.[59] The divine word, which suddenly descends into the human situation, unexpected and uncalled by humankind, fresh and free like lightning, was his mandate. And the role of the one who has to make it heard is a kind of loneliness experienced only by great poets, prophets, explorers.

Your obligation
is not discharged by any common rite.
What you must do must be done on your own.

The main thing is to write
for the joy of it ...

----

59 Karl Rahner writing in *Sacramentum Mundi, An Encycopaedia of Theology,* under the rubric Prophetism: 'The figure of the prophet, in various modifications, is a phenomenon in the history and sociology of all religions... The prophet is different from the priest, who is the minister of divine worship. Worship is in more or less set terms and gestures, its validity is established by tradition and it can be passed on to new officials in an institutionalized way. The prophet, on the contrary, always comes forward with a new message. He has to produce his own credentials. His task cannot be, strictly speaking, institutionalized... Hence the uniqueness of his vocation is essential to the prophet. He is the envoy of God. He is always to some extent the religious revolutionary, and since religion and society form a unity, he is often the critic of society.... The message which he brings is not really meant for himself alone. It is primarily for others – for those to whom he is sent with a mandate. Hence the actual nature of any given prophet must be seen as intrinsically connected with his message, with his "concept of God".' Pp 110-111.

Take off from here. And don't be so earnest,

so ready for the sackcloth and the ashes.
Let go, let fly, forget.
You've listened long enough. Now strike your note'.

It was as if I had stepped free into space
alone with nothing that I had not known
already...

'The English language/ belongs to us...

'You lose more of yourself than you redeem
doing the decent thing. Keep at a tangent.
When they make the circle wide, it's time to swim

out on your own and fill the element
with signatures on your own frequency,
echo-soundings, searches, probes, allurements,

 elver-gleams in the dark of the whole sea'.[60]

60   *Open Ground,* London, Faber, 1998, p 267-8.

CHAPTER SIX

◉

Procrustean Ethics

In Greek Mythology Procrustes, whose name means 'he who stretches', was an hotelier who lured travellers into his home near Eleusis. Procrustes pretended to offer hospitality to passing strangers. He would invite them for a sumptuous meal and a night's rest in his hostelry which contained a very special bed. This bed was widely advertised as the most comfortable and accommodating as it would adjust itself to the contours of whoever happened to lie on it. What Procrustes didn't mention to his grateful customers was the method by which this 'one-size-fits-all' was achieved. As soon as the guests lay down, Procrustes went to work, stretching them on the rack, if their body was too short; and chopping off their legs if these happened to be too long. The only reason we still hear of him is that he had the misfortune to encounter Theseus who was on his way to Athens. The myth has lingered in our imaginations and spawned many metaphorical applications.

It can describe any arbitrary standard or set of conditions to which exact conformity is required and to which everyone is forced to adjust. Wherever varying lengths, sizes or properties are fitted to one standard mould, you are said to have a procrustean arrangement. It is easy, therefore, to see why many people today regard 'morality' and 'ethics' as procrustean when these require everybody to conform to regulations which suit certain people quite naturally, but leave others thwarted and undernourished. We seem to have inherited at least two very obvious procrustean beds to which all our citizens are required to accommodate themselves: one is sociological, and will be described in Chapter Eight; the other is 'religious' and will be the subject of Chapter Seven.

The thrust of what artists are telling us is that we have created a mould for human being too narrow and too restricted. When we know the kind of people we were meant to be, we can summon up the courage and exercise the discipline necessary to achieve such a goal, which should be the moral aim of everyone. However, the paradigm of 'perfection' which Christianity, for instance, proposes to its adherents may be satisfactory for some, but it does not suit all. Morality cannot provide a 'one size fits all' formula when dealing with the multiplicity and diversity of humanity.

The ideals on which Westerners base the conduct of their lives come from European philosophy at its earliest. Most of our thinking was done for us by the Greeks. Their legacy was so solid and convincing that few thinkers coming after them gave their explanation a second thought. If the Greeks have done such a good job explaining the universe why bother to reinvent the wheel. Western European philosophy has been described as a series of footnotes to Plato. What we inherited from the Greeks was a way of life, an explanation of ourselves, an architecture for our civilisation. Most of our words to describe any of our important enterprises are Greek: politics, ethics, economy, philosophy etc. The list is almost half of our vocabulary. Every time we invent or are overwhelmed by something new we reach for a Greek word to label it. The 'tele', the 'phone', 'gamma' rays, 'micro'soft, 'paedophile', 'psychopath' are Greek words; so too are 'ethics' and 'procrustean'.

We may quite understandably think that we have changed considerably in the twenty or so centuries which separate us from the ancient Greeks, but they set the parameters and the direction so definitively, many centuries before the Christian era, that they determined both the limits and the quality of even our most recent lifestyles.

Greeks in general had a somewhat pessimistic view of our human situation: human life is not much to boast about (Republic, 486 A); all flesh is trash (Symposium 211 E); and Plato's Laws describe mortals as sheep, slaves, puppets or toys of the Gods. Plato was not just a puritan he was what Iris Murdoch[1] describes as 'a moral aristocrat', he not only regarded most of the rest of us as irretrievable in terms of 'goodness', but he saw salvation as a kind of consciousness. You pulled yourself together by getting mind to master matter. Philosophy was a spiritual discipline which allowed people to change their lives and become 'good'. In Plato's view, reason was equal to the world, able to take its measure. *The Republic* is based upon the assumption that the world can be harmonious and everything can run like clockwork. We, as human beings, can reasonably understand both ourselves and our world. The model for such a state of affairs is the clarified realm of mathematics.

The basic legacy of this Greek philosophy has been a belief that consciousness is our way to human perfection. Anything irrational is off limits. Aspects of ourselves were discounted as substandard, unworthy of our glorious title: rational animal. These pariahs to be rejected are mostly connected with our bodies. Plotinus, perhaps, after Plato and Aristotle, the greatest inventor of our Western world, was ashamed of being in the body. 'Corporeal things... belong to the kind directly opposed to the soul and present to it what is directly opposed to its essential existence'.[2] Neoplatonism, deriving from the teachings of Plotinus, influenced a large part of medieval doctrine and spirituality, especially through the writings of the so-called Pseudo-Dionysius, a [it was much later discovered] sixth century Syrian monk who was thought to be the New Testament convert of St Paul (Acts 17:34) and who deliberately forged his writings to pass as such. His merging of Neoplatonic philosophy with Christian theology received almost apostolic status because he was believed to have been a contemporary of St Paul. And although he did provide some very

1   Iris Murdoch, 'The Fire and the Sun' *Existentialists and Mystics,* ed. Peter Conradi, Chatto & Windus, London, 1997, p 403.
2   Plotinus, *Enneads,* III, 6.6.,

beautiful and fruitful guidance towards a particular school of mystical experience, he also loaded the dice very emphatically against the body, corporality and physical self-expression.

Quite naturally Greek words became the vehicle for Christianity in many of its fundamental formulations. The unwritten teachings of Jesus Christ became articulated in systems of thought which were available and apparently compatible. These are essentially Greek patterns of thought, although fed also by other sophisticated local cultures.

Over-simplified and possibly erroneous divisions grafted onto the Christian event became self-evident axioms supposedly deriving from the incarnation. God's invitation to join him in his heavenly abode was almost as dangerous to health as the procrustean invitation to the homogenizing bed. Certain protruding organs would certainly have to be lopped off.

The way you imagine you are, determines the way you decide to behave. When you believe that mind is the all important element in your make-up then you try to arrange for this one element to govern the rest. You install a monarchy and your life becomes a game of monopoly. In this regard it has been constantly stated that the head should rule the heart, that reason must govern the passions, that the soul must reign supreme over the body. Various strategies have been devised to implant this monopoly and implement this policy.

The mistake here is not so much that mind or spirit or soul should have authority and power to enslave or even destroy, but that any particular faculty or element of our make-up should be promoted to the detriment or destruction of any other. Such all-powerful hegemony of a dictatorial principle over all the rest was a choice governed by prevailing tendencies in the cultures from which it sprang; it was decisive in the development of European social and psychological history. It is a colonial bias, *carte blanche* to kill whatever refuses to submit. In such an option it is not just the choice of absolute ruler that is wrong, it is the fact of despotism itself. Everything in this strategy must lead step by step to the highest point which must be singular and from which all legitimation and authority must flow. This demands order, hierarchy, central government, arranging everything according to its own predetermined priorities. The one privileged ruler is invested with totalitarian power over all.

A distorted simplification of the complexity of humanity, an arbitrary selection of certain elements for cultivation and certain others for cauterization, the imposed authority of one particular faculty over all the rest: these provided the groundwork for the socio-cultural and psychological back-drop which became our Western heritage. An exaggerated emphasis on the 'spiritual' and a vilification of the 'physical', led also to a glorification of the conscious and a neglect of the unconscious. Reason rules and the irrational is outlawed. Such foreshortened divisions, which have caused our present schizoid culture, promoted a great divide between spirit and flesh, between soul and body, between mind and matter, between heaven and earth, between male and female.

Such simplistic topography has inhabited the European mind from the beginning of philosophy, and though the paradigms may have differed marginally and variations occurred to suit local or temporal fashion, the essential structures have remained in place. Of course, an alternative model of authority and regulation might have been found in conciliarity and consensus, for instance. Here unanimity might be achieved by dint of understanding between, and fulfilment of, each part of the composite whole in accordance with the aspiration and identity of each. This would achieve the well-being of the whole because of the satisfactory development of each particular part. Such is the effective government of an orchestra or choir as two examples; government which respects individuality and originality and has the imagination and the patience to see how these can combine to produce an unanticipated harmony. Such an alternative does not sacrifice idiosyncrasy and peculiarity to expediency and efficiency. It lets the flowers grow before it arranges the pattern of the garden. Variegated growth is encouraged rather than lopping off, or weeding out, whatever fails to conform to preordained size, shape or colour coordination.

CHAPTER SEVEN

○

The Opal and the Pearl

'Do you know what a pearl is and what an opal is? My soul when you came sauntering to me first through those sweet summer evenings was beautiful but with the pale passionless beauty of a pearl. Your love has passed through me and now I feel my mind something like an opal, that is, full of strange uncertain hues and colours, of warm lights and quick shadows and of broken music'.

This is Joyce writing to Nora on 21 August 1909.[1] The pearl and the opal are symbols of two different ways of achieving the beauty which human beings can radiate, if and when they become what they were intended to be. Such beauty is not something that we do, not something that we have; it is what we are, what we become, if we are true to our destiny. Our bodies and our faces are icons of that inner equilibrium which life can accomplish in us by a wisdom kneaded through us which leads towards integrity. 'If you're not sorted before you're seventy', a friend of mine says, 'you are likely to be a nuisance to everyone around you'. But there are at least two ways of getting 'sorted'.

Following this imagery suggested by Joyce, human perfection could be compared to an opal quite as effectively as to the more usual Christian choice of the pearl. There must be at least two ways of reaching the goal of human completion. Concentration on the one, over a two-thousand year history, has been to the detriment of the

1   *Selected Joyce Letters*, edited by Richard Ellmann, The Viking Press, New York, 1975, p 161.

other. It should not be a question of either or; it must be possible to do justice to both. Gregory of Nyssa, one of the most influential fathers of the Church, has this to say about Christian perfection:[2]

> Any action, thought or word which involves passion is out of harmony with Christ and bears the mark of the devil, who makes muddy the pearl of the soul with passions and mars the lustre of that precious jewel. That which is pure of every inclination to passion tends towards the source of all tranquillity, namely Christ.

Such writings influenced the pattern of moral education in our Western world. So much of Church teaching which we have had passed down to us through our adoption of Graeco-Roman philosophy has little to do with divine revelation. The first philosopher to write ethical treatises, Aristotle(384–322 BC), lived almost four hundred years before Jesus Christ came on earth.   Aristotle's *Nicomachean Ethics* is regarded as one of the most important historical philosophical works ever written. Its name may come from Nicomachus, who was his son [although it was also his father's name]. The treatise is the result of courses he gave for twelve years from 335 BC at the Lyceum school which he founded in Athens. The ten books, based on these lectures, which make up this treatise on ethics, could have become for him an attempt to explain to his son how he should best live his life in our strange world. It certainly became such a handbook for at least fifteen hundred years after it was written.

Aristotle taught that virtue has to do with the proper function (*ergon*) of a thing. An eye is only a good eye in so far as it can see, because the proper function of an eye is to see. Humans must also have a function specific to humans, and any such function must be,

---

2   Gregory of Nyssa, *On Christian Perfection*, PG 46, 283-286. Breviary, The Divine Office, III, Pp 224-225.

according to Aristotle, an activity of the *psyche* (normally translated as *soul*) in conjunction with reason, our most distinguishing faculty. A really successful human being will be one who is good at living life, and who does this beautifully (*kalos*). So far, so good, who could disagree? Aristotle held that the highest aim of all human practical thinking is *Eudaimonia*, a Greek word often translated as 'well-being' or happiness. Aristotelian Ethics describes what makes a virtuous character (*ethikē aretē*) possible, which in turn makes happiness possible.

A synthesis of this work, combined with Christian theology, became the most formative educational instrument by the end of the Thirteenth century in Europe. The catch-cry '*Bonum est quod omnia appetunt*' was the axiomatic first principle of all ethics and became widespread teaching, especially through the influential writings of Thomas Aquinas.[3] His work came to be understood as the definitive map of the Catholic world. His philosophy exerted enormous influence on subsequent Christian theology, especially within the Roman Catholic Church, but also extending to Western philosophy in general, where he stands as a link, although with modification, to Aristotelianism, which he fused with the thought of Augustine. His most important and enduring work is his *Summa Theologiae*, where he expounds his systematic theology embracing the reality of the whole universe and everything in it. Here in Ireland, for instance, a compact

---

3   'Unumquodque autem appetit suam perfectionem. Perfectio autem et forma effectus est quaedam similitudo agentis: cum omne agens agat sibi simile. Unde ipsum agens est appetibile, et habet rationem boni: hoc enim est quod de ipso appetitur, ut eius similitudo participetur. Cum ergo Deus sit prima causa effectiva omnium, manifestum est quod sibi competit ratio boni et appetibilis'. [Everything seeks after its own perfection, and the perfection and the form of an effect consist in a certain likeness to the agent [which caused it], since every agent makes it's like; and hence the agent itself is desirable and has the nature of good.] *Summa Theologiae*, Prima Pars, Questio VI Art. 1. The response to the second objection to this same question reads: 'All things, by desiring their own perfection, desire God Himself, inasmuch as the perfections of all things are so many similitudes of the divine being'.

resumé of this work, in *The Maynooth Catechism*, was approved by the Irish hierarchy in 1951, and was specifically intended for teaching primary-school children, required to memorize each prescribed answer by rote. Half a century of school-children, obliged to attend primary school, because benefitting from the compulsory 'free' education scheme in this country, knew no other version of what it meant to be fully alive.

The result was, and is, a very admirable and very beautiful explanation of the universe and of our role therein, which became a handbook or guide for many generations of Western European children about how we should best conduct our lives. However, it becomes dangerous and detrimental when it makes contentious judgements about who we are, about what is essential to our nature and what is not, and, above all, what an all-powerful and all-perfect God would or would not find acceptable about our humanity. Our invitation to become 'children of God', which is what Christianity was all about, when translated into a restricted and binary setting, could seem to be an invitation to renounce being human and to set about becoming divine, to stop being animals and start becoming angels. The invitation then is read as asking us to become the opposite of what we are as human beings. If 'spiritual' is interpreted as inimical to 'fleshly', for instance, then such an invitation from Divinity means renouncing or repudiating everything that is not spiritual, which might include our nature, our flesh and above all our sexuality.

This, of course, could be a very different agenda from the one which Christ's Incarnation might well have been offering. God's adoption of us as his children might have meant that our humanity was being vindicated and validated, that being fully human was being what God intended us to be, or as one of the first Christian teachers, Irenaeus, born in 130, put it: 'The Glory of God is humanity fully alive'. It could have meant that becoming fully human was synonymous with becoming holy.

This was hardly the understanding which developed as early as the second century after Christ's sojourn on our planet. The danger of so ambiguous a message as Christ preached, is that it can be interpreted according to the prejudices of the preacher. If every creature is seeking 'the good' and if 'the highest good' is the God who made us, then his invitation to join him in heaven can so easily be interpreted as renunciation of our humanity, to measure up to the sublime invitation on offer. This would further imply that our humanity is not something to be restored and revitalized in itself, it is only valuable insofar as it can become the container, the channel for God's holiness. The ambiguity here, of course, rests in the idea of what it means to be holy. Is God saying to us: 'The only way you can share in the eternal life of the Blessed Trinity is by annihilating yourself as a makeshift, impermanent and temporary creature, so that my holiness can flood through you, take you over, and make you into a durable candidate for divine life. Renunciation is the way to achieve this. Renunciation of everything that is human makes you more and more "divine".' An appeal, therefore, for the highest standards, anything less is shamed out of court. And, more ominously, if you don't accept this invitation, if you don't want to conform to its requirements, you can look forward to an eternity of punishment.

An ethics based on such over-simplified dualities must inevitably prove inadequate for many. It proposes a morality which fails to comprehend the complexity of what we are as human beings. It neither asks nor answers the questions which being or becoming human ultimately pose. When it does allow some of these questions to be asked then it might begin to move towards satisfactory and comprehensive answers which people would recognise as viable and life-promoting. Such a morality would then cease to be an 'asceticism of punitive discipline' and become what Charles Davis has called 'the asceticism of achieved spontaneity'.[4] An asceticism of punitive discipline is the

---

4   Charles Davis, *Body as Spirit*, New York, 1976, p. 53

kind of control decreed by law from central government or higher authority, imposed from above and enforced by sanction. It relies upon a systematised structure of authority and power invested in a recognized principle of government on the one hand, and fear and obedience inculcated into those receiving such orders from on high.

Asceticism of achieved spontaneity, on the other hand, is a discipline and control which emerges from a situation where each participating element recognizes the advantage to be gained and the benefits which will accrue from doing certain things in a certain way, refraining from doing others, and helping the totality of which each is a part, to achieve some goal or accomplish some feat. Such might be the discipline of athletes or musicians, for instance, as opposed to that of armies or prisons. Control of any kind, whether over others or over ourselves, can mirror either model.

When we know the kind of people we were meant to be, we can summon up the courage and exercise the discipline necessary to achieve such a goal. No one objects to renunciation which promotes life and cuts off whatever is holding us back. Renunciation as punishment, as doing to death some essential part of myself is unacceptable; renunciation as pruning towards better and more abundant growth is welcome. Renunciation of food, of pleasure, of even life itself, all these are possible; renunciation of what I am in myself is absurdity.

The word opal comes from the sanskrit úpara meaning 'lower'. It is the comparative of úpa meaning 'under', so it is the lowest of the low. At base it is a colourless silica mineral which is the principal constituent of most rocks. Disseminated impurities impart dull body colours to this undistinguished yet durable base. The so-called 'milkiness' of an opal's texture is created by an abundance of tiny gas-filled cavities. However, light causes colours to flash and change whenever the stone is viewed from different angles. The light is able to gain access through minute cracks and other internal inhomogeneities in the stone. In other words, because the stone is translucent and full of imperfections it becomes potentially colourful and thus assumes its identity as a jewel.

The pearl, on the other hand, is a more orthodox and traditional image of virtue, and is possible and available to many, even if these become fewer in number as the paradigm becomes less attractive to a less abstemious age. However unrealistic and arbitrary the model of the pearl may seem to our generation, it still can and does fashion certain exceptional individuals, who accomplish and endure a life of asceticism and restraint. However, such a programme is reserved for the gifted few and it should not be imposed, nor required for all those called to priestly ordination or so-called 'religious' life. It can only promote in the ordinary lives of most people a despairing tension. Disregard for the emotional and sexual aspect of ourselves and the other-oriented structure of our bodies and personalities may allow us to develop defence mechanisms and outer armour which help us to survive in the desert without nourishment for our philanthropic appetites; but it can also mean that we remain illiterate and undereducated in our relational faculties. Those who fail to become beautiful and impressive pearls or hermits may find themselves stumbling through the market-place of life, guilty, insecure, awkward and angry.

Pearls will always be treasured as exceptional jewels. They are the product of a defence against any invader. In Latin *pernulla* means uncontaminated, impermeable; nothing has ever penetrated the core; they are unattested; nothing has ever got through. Molluscs with double shells, such as clams, oysters and mussels, lay down pearl as the inner layer of their shells. When some foreign matter, often parasitic larva, gets into the body, the mollusc forms a small sac around the foreign body, isolating it. They then build up layer upon layer of calcium carbonate around the sac, imprisoning the invader for all time, and in the same mummifying movement they create a pearl. Natural pearls are rare. Only one oyster in a thousand contains one. Such beauty is available to a tiny minority and should not be imposed as a standard on the majority.

There are more ways to heaven than one. Option for the pearl as opposed to the opal creates role models and preferred heroes who are solitary, celibate, rugged and ascetic [and usually] male. Those of us who cannot or will not embrace and realise these ideals end up feeling second-rate and frustrated. Such programmes of perfection produce in us repressive reflexes with regard to the physical. We cultivate an ingrained fear and guilt about bodily, especially sexual, self-expression.

Rainer Maria Rilke, Joyce's contemporary in Germany, protests:

Why, I ask you, when people want to help us, who are so often helpless, why do they leave us in the lurch just there at the root of all experience? Anyone who would stand by us there could rest satisfied that we should ask nothing further from him. For the help which he imparted to us there would grow of itself with our life, becoming, together with it, greater and stronger. And would never fail. Why are we not set in the midst of what is most mysteriously ours? How we have to creep round about it and get into it in the end; like burglars and thieves, we get into our own beautiful sex, in which we lose our way and knock ourselves and stumble and finally rush out of it again, like men caught transgressing ... Why, if guilt or sin had to be invented because of the inner tension of the spirit, why did they not attach it to some other part of the body, why did they let it fall on that part, waiting until it dissolved in our pure source and poisoned and muddied it? Why have they made our sex homeless, instead of making it the place for the festival of our competency? Why do we not belong to God from this point? My sex is not directed only towards posterity, it is the secret of my own life – and it is only because it may not occupy the central place there, that so many people have thrust it to the edge, and thereby lost their balance.[5]

An exaggerated emphasis on the 'spiritual' and corresponding vilification of the carnal or physical; concentration upon self-contained identity [pearl] as contrasted with inescapable being-with-others as our inevitable situation in the world; these can colour our relationship with ourselves and with others from our very earliest years.

While in no way condemning the valid and valuable vocation of the few to the contemplative life and the life of the hermit, which we have described as the beauty of the pearl; there must be an equally valid path to fulfilment which incorporates the full gamut of our lives as full-bodied persons. Such an alternative formation, described in the image of an opal, suggests a life of contact and intimacy with others which has its own rigours, discipline and demands. Both these paths towards fulfilment require introduction, formation and education; neither come naturally to us. To become either opals or pearls we must learn to speak a quite different and very specific language. The emotional and sexual sides of ourselves must be understood as an essential part of our human growth and development. Unless our ethical philosophies include a way of negotiating all such human contact, from the most rudimentary and basic tactility right through to consummated orgasmic communion, they fall short of the comprehensive inclusivity required of a comprehensive morality.

The suggestion that Christian, especially Catholic, orthodoxy is irrevocably aligned with the first of these attitudes, must be eschewed. Christian teaching and principles may well advance and promote the morality prescribed in the life of the pearl, but these can only be undermined and reviled if they are not complemented and counterbalanced by the equally valuable morality of the opal.

5   Rainer Maria Rilke, 'The Young Workman's Letter' [February 1922] translated in *Rodin and Other Prose Pieces* (London, 1986) Pp 151-152.

If we are faced with a choice between supposedly 'Christian' values and more contemporary 'heretical' discoveries we create once again oppositions entirely of our own making. These were never meant to be pitted against each other, certainly not by the founder of Christianity. No one has the right or the mandate to deprive Christianity of any aspect of our humanity. Everything we discover about ourselves should be integrated into our Christian anthropology, so that 'in the end', as Rilke says, whatever route we take, 'we shall have been marvellously prepared for divine relationship'.

CHAPTER EIGHT

○

Adam and Eve and Pinch me

Adam and Eve and Pinch me
Went down to the river to bathe
Adam and Eve were drowned
And who do you think was saved?

This is a game we used to play as children and, of course, who-ever got the right answer and said 'Pinch me!' was rounded upon and pinched black and blue. But now it's time to stop playing this game and to pinch ourselves properly and wake up. The Adam and Eve dream, if taken literally, becomes a nightmare, and one which we have all been living for too long, to our cost. In our society, right up to the twenty-first century, you only have to be born to be slotted into either category, and the determining colours were pink and blue: pink for a girl and blue for a boy. Girls get dolls, crochet sets, and cooking utensils in their Christmas stockings; boys get tractors, tin soldiers and guns. Education is the process which supplies children with the cultural canopy woven by the particular tribe into which they happen to be born. By the age of one we are picking up gender signals from all around us. I am a man, I had better behave like this; you are a woman, this is your preferred set of reactions.

We are dealing here with a problem that is as old as humankind itself. We keep on hearing of ancient civilizations, including our own Celtic forbears, who were not male chauvinists but had a balanced and egalitarian attitude towards women. And we are told about the pre-history of far-of islands in the Pacific, where women ruled the roost. Experts in various fields of ethnology have described such analyses as romantic projection of idealised scenarios upon what is, at best, indecipherable evidence. The facts, unfortunately, seem to point towards universal domination of the bully boys in the school yard during the known history of the universe, and a consistent hatred for the feminine, whether in ourselves or in others.

Men have always dominated and masculinity has at all times and in all places usurped the feminine. This universal human phenomenon which has impoverished our planet so radically is nothing less than the indiscriminate crushing out of the feminine principle.

We have been made aware of a tendency in our humanity towards genocide which the twentieth century made so flagrantly transparent that we had to do something about it. International tribunals were established to punish perpetrators, where these could be found, and a case proven against them. What we have not yet been made aware of is the tendency towards 'gynecide'. This is my own invented term for the equivalent to 'genocide', where the 'race' to be wiped out are the women of the species. 'Gyne' in Greek means 'woman'; 'cide' comes from the Latin 'caedere' meaning to kill. Gynecide is then the universal attempt to purge ourselves and our planet of the feminine principle. This seemingly innate tendency in our species has led not just towards worldwide sexism, which we are beginning to redress slowly but surely, we hope, but it has also meant the violent hatred for, and extirpation of, any manifestation of the feminine inside the male variety itself.

Again we seem to have made a false division: cutting the world into two halves which we choose to call 'men' and 'women'. We have to begin to understand and recognise that there is a huge variety of gender, infinite and complicated permutations of both male and female, even within each one of us. Until we begin, as a society, to understand and to celebrate this kaleidoscope of possibility in every new human being we bring into the world, we are unlikely to provide them with a comfortable identity. There is an ever-growing percentage of people in physical bodies which contradict their socially determined gender group. Not everyone identifies as male or female. Chris Ricketts describes a journey from gender confusion to self-acceptance.[1] Chris always knew that she didn't fit comfortably into either category, and her doctors agreed. But 'she rejected the radical surgery and hormone therapy she was offered, because she felt there was nothing about her that needed to be reassigned. Instead she went on a spiritual journey to find her place in a world that appeared to have no place for her'.

In Canada Kathy Witterick and her partner Derek Stocker made a radical choice in terms of their child. When Storm was four months old only a handful of people know his/her gender, including his/her brothers, 5-year-old Jazz and 2-year-old Kio. His/her sex was not in question, the parents simply wanted to shield the baby from society's preoccupation with gender rules. Two years later, only a small circle knows if Storm is a boy or a girl. The family is a genderless home, to the extent that such is possible, or that genders are fluid. But society feels threatened by any such variation. This story provoked an international protest, accusing the parents of conducting a social experiment on their children.

Whatever the practical solutions, we must accept that we have made too categorical and unequivocal a divide between male and female. Our cultures have undervalued and degraded the feminine, both as internal part of each one of us, and as incarnated in over 50% of the human race registered as women. We should no longer make such stark divisions between the two genders but should recognize the continuity of the spectrum in which we all share, in varying degrees. Each of us is situated somewhere along a spectrum of masculine and feminine traits and characteristics, making each of our particular identities as unique and unrepeatable as a finger-print.

1   Chris Ricketts, *Food Needs Labelling, People Don't*, Little Singing Bear, Dublin, 2016

Has any progress been made now that we are in the second decade of the twenty-first century? Only if we recognize the cauldron of change which was the twentieth century.

Nothing much happened, it has to be said, until the twentieth century. Whatever else occurred in that hundred years, which many might say were the most horrific of recorded history, major steps were taken in the direction of parity between women and men, and validation of the feminine in every walk of life. And again, nothing would have happened without determined effort on the part of far-seeing and courageous pioneers who launched the cause of feminism in sometimes overwhelmingly antagonistic circumstances.

First Wave Feminism in the early twentieth century focused mainly on women's suffrage, basic rights, political franchise. What we accept now as completely normal only became law in England in 1928, for instance. The struggle to achieve even such minimal presence in public life had to be heroic. What we might call Second Wave Feminism of the 1960s concerned basic health issues and gender equality, most importantly in the areas of law and culture. Reform of the first copperfastens change in the more nebulous atmosphere of the second. Whereas the first wave evinced a reaction of political as well as physical violence on the part of the establishment, the second wave was more subtle and less visible, taking place at a social, psychological and ideological level. There were powerful protagonists on both sides. A megaphone battle of the sexes ensued throughout Europe and America. Both sides were well represented but the battle itself did little to pour oil on troubled waters. An aggressive set-to made it difficult for either side to back down or achieve reconciliation.

Third Wave feminism of the 1990s was less reactive, and placed more focus on developing talents and achievements of women within a more tempered strategy. This engaged greater numbers of people, some of whom might have been alienated by the more aggressive tactics and supremacist goals of earlier times. Without these forerunners, however, nothing would have changed. But we cannot pretend that the battle has not taken place nor can we deny that the world has been moved on however much in spite of itself. Of course we can, and some of us do, refuse to accept the new situation. We can refuse to move into the twenty-first century and bed ourselves down in the nineteenth as if the hundred years of the twentieth had never taken place. We may even feel that such a reactionary stance is a positive one, that all the innovations in the meantime have been negative, even evil. Such a jaundiced view of the present requires a more critical survey of the past.

There is little doubt that the patriarchal society of the last two-to four-thousand years, with its excess of male power and energy, has been responsible for many of the world's current problems: ruthless pursuit of power, destructive exploitation of the natural world, insanity of nuclear weapons, violence between nations, denigration of women, child abuse, racial oppression, isolating competitiveness and soulless materialism. And in this system, it must be admitted, there are women who are, and have been, quite as ruthless as men. However, as of now, in most developed countries, the majority have come to accept that, at every level of our socio-political structured life, the percentage of female participation should increase to tipping-point if any radical change for the better, and especially for equality and parity between men and women, is to take place. This is not simply a numbers game, it is about the quality of life which all governance is there to effect.

If such 'men' remain in charge, if such a psychology is deemed essentially and biologically 'masculine', then it is no wonder that women are appalled by the reality that only 12% of those working in the higher echelons of computer technology, for instance, are women. What kind of monsters are the male psyche likely to produce, and what kind of world are they likely to usher in for our children. Men do not ask themselves questions, some analysts tell us, about the likely results or consequences of their investigations and experimentation; they concern themselves simply with what can be achieved, with what combinations can be elucidated, with what the furthest horizons of our inventive powers can accomplish. Such uncontrolled and irresponsible craving for novelty, at the control board of the most advanced technological capacity to create should give us pause.

In laboratories throughout the world, scientists are learning how to engineer living beings. They can break any law of so-called natural selection with impunity, without even a thought for an organism's original characteristics. For instance, Eduardo Kac, a Brazilian bio-artist, [living in Chicago] decided in 2000 to create a fluorescent green rabbit. He contacted a French laboratory and offered to pay them to engineer a green rabbit according to his specification. The geneticist, Louis-Marie Houdebine, took an ordinary white rabbit embryo, implanted in its DNA a gene taken from a green fluorescent jellyfish, and produced, as a combination, the rabbit called Alba. The lifespan, or indeed quality of life, of the new creation hardly concerned the laboratory technicians. In 2002, a US reporter made contact with INRA (French National Institute for Agricultural Research), where Houbedine works, and was told that Alba had died. The only evidence provided was a quote from Houbedine: "I was informed one day that bunny was dead. So, rabbits die often. It was about 4 years old, which is a normal lifespan in our facilities".[2]

A balance between these two tendencies should be achieved and maintained, even if this has never been done before. The human species is in charge of its own cultural development. It is not like the animal kingdom, prisoner to the laws of its nature, to the instinctive coding in its DNA. We can invent whatever culture we choose to endorse, provided we have the collective will to do so. But to do so we must change our paradigms. The suggestion that because there are

2   http://www.genomenewsnetwork.org/articles/03_02/bunny_art.shtml.

two forms of the one species, male and female, our culture must be either matriarchy or patriarchy, that either the women must dominate the men or vice versa, is simply to transfer the worst features of the culture of the past onto all culture of the future. Domination is the hall-mark of the patriarchal paradigm. It should be replaced by a paradigm of partnership.

Time journalist Jay Newton-Small, in her book, *Broad Influence*, argues that once women's participation reaches at least 20% of a group, they can 'change the culture and influence outcomes'. Women bring particular skills and perspectives, including facility to communicate and propensity to listen, readiness to compromise, and ability to form alliances. Their presence is a game changer.[3]

Each country, including our own, should do statistical analyses to find out where we stand on the spectrum of such percentages. Here in Ireland for the first time in 2017 there are more women solicitors than men. This is a first for any legal profession in the world. However, Senator Averil Power holds that figures for female representation in parliament place us 'way behind parts of Sub-Saharan Africa'.[4]

The elephant in the room is the Roman Catholic Church where there is no female participation at the level of government. Over the two thousand-year history of the Church as an institution, not only women but lay persons generally have had a very limited profile. Priestly anointing is deemed necessary for legitimate exercise of divine power. You either have that power or you don't, and the only way to plug into this source is through priestly ordination. The logic at least is consistent.

The Catholic Church is the oldest religious institution in existence. It has over one billion members living in almost every country in the world. In its own eyes it is a divinely appointed institution, perennially

---

3   Jay Newton-Small, *Broad Influence: How Women are Changing the Way America Works*, New York, Time Books, 2016.
4   *Irish Independent*, Saturday Review, 6/2/2016, p. 2

guided by the Holy Spirit. It was founded by God, who came on earth in the person of Jesus Christ for thirty-three years to institute it. He handed over his authority to twelve apostles, headed by Peter, the first of now two hundred and sixty-six popes who have presided over those two thousand years. Pope Francis I is the two hundred and sixty-sixth Pope since 13 March 2013. Historical evidence suggests that this Church is also a fully human organization which travels through history as a dweller on this planet, and is therefore prey to all the deficiencies and shortcomings of any such institutions. Crimes and horrors have been perpetrated by its members and in its name. However, in spite of the aberrant behaviour of many of Christianity's adherents, the truth which it embodies and which is its direct source and origin is still the truth that can save us and save our world. And by 'save' is meant accomplish for us, in us, through us, the highest form of life possible to imagine, both now and in eternity. That is the ultimate truth which gives us hope and allows us to adhere to a religion which others might find obsolete, if not even evil. And in case there should be any doubt about the Catholic Church's capacity to guide the faithful along the right path towards salvation, the First Vatican Council of 1869–1870, declared, as a dogma to be believed henceforth by all Catholics, the infallibility of the Pope, which means that when the reigning Pope 'defines' *ex cathedra*', that is in the discharge of his office as shepherd and teacher of all Christians, and by virtue of his supreme apostolic authority, that a doctrine concerning faith or morals must be held by the whole Church, then this is an infallible pronouncement binding all Catholics.

The principal document outlining the Church's teaching on the ordination of women, *Inter Insigniores*, was published by the Congregation of the Doctrine of the Faith, in October 1976. The teaching was reconfirmed by Pope John Paul II in his Apostolic Letter *Ordinatio Sacerdotalis*, of May 1994. He put in an addendum (n.4) that this was not just a disciplinary matter, open to further debate, but was a 'judgement to be definitely held by all the Church's faithful'.

The main argument in both documents is that 'the Church, in fidelity to the example of the Lord, does not consider herself authorized to admit women to priestly ordination' (*Inter Insigniores*, Introduction). This argument is based on the fact that Jesus called only men to be part of the twelve, that the early apostolic community maintained this 'men only' norm, as did the subsequent tradition down through the ages. The document maintains that the practice of Jesus 'was not in order to conform to the customs of his time, for his attitude towards women was quite different from that of his milieu, and he deliberately and courageously broke with it'. *Inter Insigniores* acknowledges that contemporary questions concerning the ordination of women are posed in a way 'which classical theology scarcely touched upon'. However its conclusion is couched in absolute terms, repeated by John Paul II: 'I declare that the Church has no authority whatsoever to confer priestly ordination on women' (OS, 4). Despite the solemnity of the language, theological opinion is clear that we do not have here infallible teaching.[5]

Four years as Pope at the time of writing this book, Francis continues to confound. His simplicity, his charm, his authenticity are patent, and people can tell that his heart is in the right place. He has a pastoral concern for ordinary people and an open unguarded fluency when in conversation with those he meets. All this is wonderful, and most well-meaning people love his style. But there must be more than that, and the next few years will tell the story. Can he effect the changes in the Church which he has so eloquently articulated in his Apostolic Exhortation on the Proclamation of the Gospel in To-day's World, *Evangelii Gaudium*, which acts as a clarion call for 'a pastoral and missionary conversion which cannot leave things as they

5   Gerry O'Hanlon S.J., 'Church, Women, Authority, Why Not?' *Doctrine & Life*, Vol 66, No 1, January, 2016, Pp. 33-45.

presently are' (#25). Can he get the Catholic Church to 're-examine' various 'rules or precepts' and 'certain customs' when 'considering a reform of the Church'. There are powerful forces working against this possibility. And, like everyone, he has his limitations. Coming from South America he may not share the hopes and aspirations of European Catholics, especially women. Francis told reporters when returning from Brazil in September 2013: 'With regards to the ordination of women, the Church has spoken and says no. Pope John Paul [II] said so with a formula that was definitive. That door is closed'.

Many people today find it impossible to accept any such ruling. Democracy is the idiom of most civilized countries, and educated people are not just used to having their voices heard, but they regard it as their basic right to have a say in all important matters which concern their well-being. We, living as we do, in a Western European society have no difficulty seeing that women are perfectly entitled to, and capable of, any position of power or exercise of authority. Angela Merkel, Mary Robinson, Mary McAleese, to mention a few, have banished for us the mirage and mythology of male supremacy in any order or field. But we are a small proportion of the geography and the personnel which make up the 1.2 billion Catholics around the globe. In many areas of this constituency little progress has been made in terms of women's liberation.

Robert McClory has an interesting take on the last sentence of Pope Francis quoted above: 'Definitive' and 'infallible' are not the same thing. A door is not a wall. Anyone can open a door if they have the key.[6] There are powerful forces working against this slim possibility. Can one man pit himself against the deeply entrenched conservatism of one of the largest and the oldest religious institutions in the world?

....

6   Robert McClory, 'Pope Francis and Women's Ordination', *The National Catholic Reporter*, September 16th 2013. http://ncronline.org/blogs/ncr-today/pope-francis-and-womens-ordination.

Pope Francis in an exchange with Fr Antonio Spadaro, SJ, editor in chief of La Civiltà Cattolica,[7] has also said: 'the feminine genius is needed wherever we make important decisions'. That's fine but 'Only if we break through the theological mystifications and religious legitimisations of patriarchal authority and power will women be able to reclaim our dignity, authority and power as ecclesial subjects'.[8] A theological opinion about 'sacred power', not sufficiently debated by theologians, has become standard and has been incorporated into the Revised Code of Canon Law (1983), in particular in Canon 129, says Ladislas Orsy, an expert in Canon Law. This canon specifies that those who have received sacred orders are qualified for the power of governance, also called the power of jurisdiction; lay members of the Christian faithful can cooperate in the exercise of this same power, but 'cooperate' does not mean 'participate'.This has not always been the case, but it is now irrevocable unless this recent incorporation into the revised code is rescinded. Women have not always been so excluded from governance. The Empress Irene both convoked and presided over parts of the Second Council of Nicaea in 787 CE.[9]

What will happen, what can happen to redress such imbalance? Our world is precariously poised, metaphorically speaking, on two tectonic plates as far as socio-political awareness is concerned. On the one hand you have the more advanced and sophisticated cultures, such as many of us in the so-called 'first-world' enjoy, where democracy has become the accepted idiom. Then you have the Catholic Church, and many others who, in certain respects, have not yet moved out of the nineteenth century. But, at this time, is as if these two tectonic plates are on the move. The place where they could

7   English translation of this interview which took place 19th August, 2013, in *America* (30 September, 2013).
8   Elizabeth Schüssler Fiorenza, 'Claiming our Authority and Power', *Concilium*, (180) 1985, p 50.
9   Gerard Mannion, 'Changing the (Magisterial) Subject: Women Teaching-with-Authority – from Vatican II to Tomorrow,' Irish Theological Quarterly, Volume 81, no 1, February 2016, p 17, footnote 52.

meet is called a *plate boundary*. Plate boundaries are commonly as-sociated with geological events such as earthquakes. In this instance, the plate boundary could well be Ireland where we have one section of our people living in the third decade of the twenty-first century and another portion planted squarely on the other tectonic plate in the nineteenth. When previous tectonic plates separated, the cliffs of Moher on the west coast of Ireland represented one half of the divide and Nova Scotia in Canada became the other, with the Atlan-tic Ocean in between. We may have to experience an even greater divide if the two tectonic plates I have been describing collide before the Church realises that such danger is imminent. Dr David Barker responsible for the 2004 Report of the Church in America, refers to the 'perceived wisdom that culture change takes two hundred years in the Church'. 'This is no longer an acceptable point of view; it is an excuse for inaction', he warns. The Catholic Church in Ireland has probably five or, at most, ten years before being reduced to a tiny minority.

Conclusion

Times have changed; both the world and ourselves are different from what they were one hundred years ago. We need different strategies, policies, norms and behavioural patterns, to live together in harmony, not just as one tiny island community, but as part of an ever-expanding and, at the same time, interconnecting universe. The twentieth century was a crucible. The world which has emerged from this time-machine is changed, changed utterly. There is no going back; our only way is forward. Discovery of the world of the unconscious; full acknowledgement and acceptance of the dimension of femininity, both inside and outside of ourselves, with all this implies in terms of gender balance and sexual diversity; recognition of the immensity of scientific discovery; and humble apprenticeship in a laboratory of ever-expanding technology; these are some of the characteristics required for access, capability and survival in the new world we have inherited.

Of course it is possible to remain stubbornly ensconced in a preferred world of the past, to batten down the hatches and create an 'old-world' milieu for ourselves and those who care to join us, but such a King Canute-like attitude can only be a holding operation, the waves of change must always eventually submerge even the most resolute dug-out.

There can be no general principles guiding our countries approach to participation in global citizenship, each country has to work their way according to their particular situation within the network. However, as a small country with a hundred-year-old history of independence we certainly have to decide whether we intend to work from a nineteenth or a twenty-first century template. And certainly for anyone claiming to be 'Catholic' refusal to embrace universality must go against the thrust of conviction that His salvation should reach to the ends of the earth. It is important not to allow the perception of a reactionary ghettoized minority to be foisted upon us by the media and some hostile public opinion. The world itself is the universal religion that precedes all organized religions. Nature is the first scripture wherein we read the word of God. If we want to find an icon of the face of God we will find it in the face of every single person we meet, all made in God's image and likeness,

And, we have to face reality; another unfortunate but understandable difficulty is that the word 'Catholic' can have bad press in the twenty-first century thanks to catastrophic revelations of evil-doing in the recent past, which has undermined trust in the institution as such. Banner headlines, cartoons and caricatures, depict The Catholic Church, for the Pantomime which the Press is keen to promote, as Wicked Stepmother of every fairy tale, Cruella de Vil, or the strict governess in General Montgomery's autobiography who used to get up every morning and say: 'Go out and see what that child is doing and stop him!'

If we wish to remain conservative and old-fashioned, at least let us not be sectarian and supportive of values and lifestyles which have been rejected by the majority of twenty-first century families. Otherwise we are categorized as out-of-date leftovers from a previous era, such as the Amish communities in America and Canada. These were founded in the seventeenth century and they steadfastly refuse on principal to move into the twenty-first. They use horses for farming and transportation, dress in a traditional manner and forbid electricity or telephones in the home. Church members do not join the military, nor do they apply for Social Security benefits. They refuse to take out insurance or accept any form of financial assistance from the government. They value rural life, manual labour and humility, and they discontinue formal education at the age of fourteen. We might be less identifiable and less obvious retros but nonetheless determined to remain behind where the nineteenth century left off.

It is not for us or for anyone else to create a new world. Nor can our task be that of supplying a 'world-view'. There is a real world out there which is always more than my vision of, or even my perspective on, it. There is a new-born child who enters that world, and who may be the one who is going to provide us all with an insight never before imagined. Our job is not to obscure, to hide or to pretend there is another one; our job is to make an introduction, make a connection between that child and the world we both live in, without second guessing the conclusion, or pre-empting the possible result. Anything can happen when personhood meets the universe.

Of course we should try to make the best possible introduction and provide an overview, but these should be fair-minded and realistic, not dogmatic or overly prescriptive. Values should be stressed rather than rules or ethical regulations. We need to introduce a 'gyroscopic ethics', which is my own phrase for a morality somewhere between old-style ethics based on 'natural law' or other absolute principles, and the pragmatic relativity of 'situation ethics'. Others have called this in-between an 'artistic ethics' which would require imagination above everything else.[1]

Much of the social pathology which contaminated Ireland in the twentieth century sprang from a spiritual and moral paradigm forced upon us as an island of 'Saints and Scholars'. Some of us were, and more credit to them; but the majority were not; and these were damaged by the attempt to force them into this mould. The ideals on which we based the conduct of our lives may have been very noble but they did not represent us as we are. Unless such sociology acknowledges and integrates our full humanity, we become dislocated, schizoid,

---

1   Mark Johnson, *Moral Imagination, Implications of Cognitive Science for Ethics*, University of Chicago, 1993.

two-timers. Our job now is to prepare an alternative possibility for being human, which can work for ourselves and for our children, in a new century. If we deny the reality of what we are, and set ourselves a corresponding programme of completion, the unacknowledged half of our make-up, which has been overlooked or neglected, will eventually break away and lead a maverick life of its own. *The Strange Story of Dr Jekyll and Mr Hyde* was Robert Louis Stevenson's way of describing such a possibility. If, like Mr Rochester, in Charlotte Brontë's *Jane Eyre*, we lock up our disturbed wife in the attic, and pretend to ourselves and to everyone else that she does not exist, eventually she will escape, creep out at night, and burn the house down.

The novel, as an art form, can act as defender of the orthodoxy of our humanity. We want to be human, fully human. The job of the artist is to describe that reality as it actually is. Artists have been doing that from the beginning and because they have been doing so they have been condemned. We prefer the model we have conjured to the reality we have abjured. Now that we have legislated for gay marriage and accepted the fact that sexuality does happen for reasons other than procreation; now that we also recognize that some of the most heinous sexual crimes have been perpetrated within the 'sanctity' of marriage; it is surely time to take a more comprehensive approach to the ethics of sexual behaviour. Every or any sexual activity can be good or evil, and the act itself right through to the moment of orgasm is always somewhere on a spectrum between selfish egotism and altruistic communion. This is what Iris Murdoch attempts to show in the laboratory of her many novels.

Sex in Ireland was only talked about in the context of the natural law of God and confined to religious discourse.[2] It is time to have a conversation with our intestines and a reality check on our ideals. This conversation has been initiated for us by many artists in

---

2   Diarmaid Ferriter, *Occasions of Sin, Sex & Society in Modern Ireland*, Profile Books, London, 2009, p. 24.

different media. These can become a kickstart for that essential dialogue with ourselves. What Nora was for James Joyce, a trustworthy, non-judgmental, understanding partner, many others have had to stumble upon in brothels or with people they have paid for such, more or less, successful reciprocity. The purpose of the conversation is to articulate the contours of our deepest longings and desires whether this happens verbally or gesturally.

What we can also learn from artists is that the ache of such deep longing and desire can be assuaged symbolically, especially when we are in the second half of our life, rather than having to express it literally or factually. Artistic self-expression can satisfactorily appease the inner tensions of our being, if we can find the proportionate and adequate alternative receptacle wherewith and wherein to articulate and contain such energy. Compulsive acting out of unresolved instinctual impulses can be channelled into more creative and productive outlets by humble acknowledgement and accurate description [analysis].

There has been little attempt to explain, to train, to encourage or to mature, the relational, emotional or sexual life of our people. In the past it was as if such life did not exist, or needed no training, direction, understanding. It was presumed that it arrived fully fledged in the marriage bed, the only location where its practice was permitted. Even the most basic courses on love-making teach that a man has to train himself to prevent orgasm occurring prematurely before it can be shared with his partner. This does not come naturally. On the contrary, the natural orgasm and ejection of sperm for a man is unencumbered and immediate. That is the biological way, the optimum performance in terms of procreation and reproduction of the species. But in order to humanize that instinct and introduce its relational dimension, causing tenderness, mutuality and reciprocity to imbue it with their celebrated meaning, people have to be told, have to listen, have to be humble apprentices to love. Lovers have to learn, discipline themselves, and gain a control which will help them to be sexual in a way that makes them sensitively reciprocal. Otherwise sexuality is the tool of selfish individuality and autistic monologue.

It is too easy and too obtuse to claim that you have solved all problems of sexuality by declaring that only those who have been married as man and woman, either legally or sacramentally or both, are entitled to engage in sexual relationship with each other; that the primary purpose of sexuality is procreation of children; that any sexual activity which precludes this possibility is prohibited; that all sexual engagement outside the bonds of marriage is sinful. Does such a sweeping overview imply that once you are married no holds are barred; that any kind of sexual activity is permitted simply because there can be no legitimate supervision of the nuptial chamber once the married couple have gained access. Does it imply that all sexual activity of whatever kind is condemned outside that prescribed sanctuary.

It is as if in an airport you tried to confine all sneezing to those with a premium pass to the business class lounge. Outside that sanctum no sternutation. Those who are trying to establish an essentially human character to every aspect of sexual behaviour must realise what statistics suggest: many of our young people have engaged in some form of sexual activity by the age of thirteen. It is time to establish an alternative ethics for the carnal community.

It must be possible, at a personal level, to trace our own particular history in terms of sexual relationship, measuring the combinations of motivation and performance in varying degrees of exploitation, adventure, domination, infatuation, lust, compassion, generosity and love, to name but a few of the possible ingredients. More importantly, it should be possible to 'humanize' this essential aspect of our being so that it ceases to be an uncontrolled exercise of selfish gluttony and realises its potential as the climax of inter-personal communion. Such understanding and achievement requires humility and honesty in assessing our cravings and our capacities, in this fraught area of our most intimate being, and then our preparedness to undergo training and education where we have too often been too shamefaced and too ravenous to see the need for any such.

At the other end of the sexual spectrum is the possibility of becoming that kind of sexual being who relates to God. The word 'monk' comes from the Greek 'monos' meaning 'alone', 'solitary', 'sole', or 'single'. You are meant to live on your own with God.

St Anthony, who moved to the desert in 270–271, became known as both the father and founder of desert monasticism. By the time he died in 356, thousands of monks and nuns had been drawn to living in the desert following his example. From the third century in the deserts of Egypt, monks and nuns could be found, and people visited them to seek advice or learn from their wisdom. The *Apophthegmata*, a collection of the sayings of some of these early desert monks and nuns, is still in print and very much in use, translated as *Sayings of the Desert Fathers and Mothers*. These hermits of the desert had a major influence on the development of Christianity. Those who left for the desert formed an alternate Christian society, at a time when it was no longer a risk to be a Christian. Anthony viewed desert solitariness as a way to focus one's attention on refining and purifying the spirit. Thousands joined him in the desert. By the time of Anthony's death, there were so many men and women living in the desert that it was described as a city by Anthony's biographer.

In the spirituality of these monks of the desert 'sexual desire revealed the knot of unsurrendered privacy' that lay at the very heart of the human person. This meant that 'sexuality became an ideogram of the unopened heart'. Purity of heart was accomplished through revealing to another the fullest account of your secret thoughts and desires. 'Sexual lapses were a fact of desert life. Monks were known to have become fathers of sons. Older monks harassed the novices... Bestiality with the monastery's donkeys could not be ruled out'. The content of all these thoughts and desires was as irrelevant as it was extravagant. The important thing was the humility and the trust which allowed you to express all this fully to another person who could then become your spiritual father or mother, capable of changing the desert where nothing can grow into a place where growth can flourish. The monks became gardeners of the desert of the heart. 'The abatement of sexual fantasy in the heart of the monk – an abatement that was held to be accompanied, quite concretely, with the cessation of the monk's night emissions – signalled, in the body, the ascetic's final victory over the closed heart... The sexuality of the emission created a disjunction between the public, daylight self and the last oasis of incommunicable, privatised experience'.[3]

Why did sexuality come to occupy such a critical position and bear such weight for the monks in the desert?

> The body, in which sexuality lurked with such baffling tenacity, had come to be viewed in the searching light of a new, high hope: 'What is this mystery in me? What is the purpose of this mixture of body and soul?''Everyone should struggle to raise his clay, so to speak, to a place on the throne of God.'

> The desert became the powerhouse of a new culture. Origen's spirituality remained that of an urban study group... It was the precise meaning of Scripture, pondered by highly literate men and women, that caused the heart of the Christian 'to burn'... In the Life of Anthony, and in successive layers of spiritual guidance, we can detect the emergence of an alternative. The monk's heart was the new book. What required infinitely skilled exegesis and long spiritual experience were 'movements of the heart', and strategies and snares that the Devil laid within it.

3   Peter Brown, *The Body and Society*, New York, 1988, Pp 229-231.

Examination of the heart was not something to be undertaken on one's own. A suitable partner had to be found. 'such movements were best conveyed orally to a spiritual father'.

> The shift from a culture of the book to a *Cultura Dei* based largely on the non-literate verbal exchange of a monastic 'art of thought' was rightly hailed as the greatest and the most peculiar achievement of the Old Men of Egypt: it amounted to nothing less than the discovery of a new alphabet of the heart.

'The aim of spiritual guidance' in the spirituality of the desert, 'was the total expropriation of the inner world of the disciple. The inner world must be turned inside out'. At this level, sexual thoughts served as 'barium traces by which the Desert monks mapped out the deepest and most private recesses of the will'.

Every religion that seriously proposes full-time contemplation as a way of life has identified 'celibacy' as the appropriate way of redirecting energy in the direction of the divine. This happens when that energy is focused upon and directed towards the base of the spine and allowed to travel upwards to the area of the brain. Meditation techniques of various kinds, involving posture and concentration and, as in tantric religion, exercises in sexual continence, which include sexual intercourse without reaching orgasm, have been devised the world over to help lovers of God to become 'theosexuals'. Just as it is possible for athletes and astronauts to train themselves to make their bodies perform in a way, to an extent and in a particular direction that seems impossible and unnatural, so the person who freely chooses to love in this way can focus themselves in the direction of the divine in a way that changes their total orientation.

Recent studies in neurobiology have suggested that the human brain, at its highest point is not so much a definite structure in itself as a kind of plasticity awaiting the arrangement which the particular person wishes to impress upon it. We are capable of completing the creation that we are by developing our brain in such a way that it becomes the appropriate receptacle for the kind of life I wish to lead, and the promotor of the kind of person I decide to become.

I believe in the possibility of celibacy and the condition of Christian chastity as fulfilling ways of being in relationship with each other and with God, but I don't believe that everyone who wants to devote their life to God should be required to be celibate. This is very particular way of being. It requires not just understanding and training, but a desire and a capacity to follow it as a way of life. Contemplatives in every religious tradition have always associated the most sublime connection with God with celibacy. Such a condition does not always take the shape of a pearl. There are at least as many opals who have also made this connection and remained steadfast. The opal and the pearl can be found anywhere in the world including monasteries.

Underground Cathedrals

(COLUMBA PRESS, €14.99) ISBN: 9781856076951

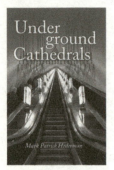

'My proposal is that, at this time, the Holy Spirit is unearthing an underground cathedral in Ireland which could help to replace the pretentious, over-elaborate Irish Catholic architecture of the twentieth century.'

Coupled with very incisive and honest comments on the current state of the church, and with a reflective meditation on the Murphy Report on the Dublin Archdiocese, Abbot Hederman offers a visionary and very stimulating image of how things might be if only we all listen to the voices of artists in our midst.

Dancing with Dinosaurs

(COLUMBA PRESS, €9.99) ISBN: 9781856077354

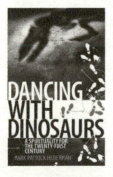

Dinosaurs have been described as the most successful animals that ever inhabited this planet. We had to learn how to live with them, and survive in spite of them. Today we have invented our own dinosaurs. Churches, banks and multinationals are some of the modern breed of dinosaur. Small may be beautiful, but in the world in which we live it is not very durable. Unless any organisation becomes a dinosaur it will not survive the vicissitudes of history.

Apocalypse of Clay - Desmond Swan

(CURRACH PRESS, €19.99) ISBN: 9781782188261

Patrick Kavanagh's epic poem The Great Hunger, published in 1942, is regarded as his greatest achievement. Apocalypse of Clay illuminates Kavanagh's prophetic insights in this bleak poem, his diagnosis of an emotional malaise at the heart of Irish society itself, which in innocence was disregarded but which would give rise to abuses in Church, society and family that would only come to light two generations later. Over its seventy-one years, the poem, has gained near unanimous critical acclaim, with Seamus Heaney, for instance calling it 'a masterpiece'.

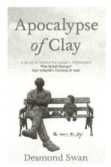

Joyce County – Ray Burke

(CURRACH PRESS, €19.99) ISBN: 9781782188858

This book by RTÉ's head of News, Ray Burke, is the first to ever look closely at the influence that Galway had on James Joyce. Written in accessible style for the general reader rather than the Joycean specialist, the book contains considerable new information, such as the first detailed account of the suspicious grounding of a passenger ship in Galway Bay in 1858, an event which gripped Joyce's imagination and features in Ulysses. It also gives fresh insights into Nora Barnacle's influence on Joyce's writings and his relationship with his tragic only daughter Lucia, 'a granddaughter of Galway'.

All books are available to order directly from www.currach.ie